TODAY'S GOOD NEWS

General Editor: The Rev. David Field
Consulting Editors: The Rev. John Stott
The Rev. Dr Leighton Ford

What is Love?

I0834976

in the same series

BORN INTO BATTLE Eddie Gibbs
THE MAN WHO SAID 'NO' Geoff Treasure
THAT'S LIFE! Chris Sugden
THE WAY OUT Andrew Knowles
GOD'S FRIENDS Michael Saward
ACT IT OUT David Field

What is Love?

Hosea

KEVIN LOGAN

Illustrated by Annie Vallotton

Collins/Fount Paperbacks

Church Pastoral Aid Society
Falcon Books

First published in Fount Paperbacks 1978
Text © Kevin Logan 1978
Illustrations © Collins/Falcon Books
Good News Bible, Today's English Version:
Old Testament © American Bible Society,
New York, 1976

British usage edition reproduced here by kind
permission of the British & Foreign Bible Society

Made and printed in Great Britain by
William Collins Sons & Co Ltd, Glasgow

CONTENTS

Doing what you're told (1:1-2:1)   7

Trusting him with your life (2:2-17)   17

A never-say-die affair (2:2-17)   24

Taking her back (2:18-3:5)   29

Letting justice be done (4:1-19)   36

Knowing who's in charge (5:1-15)   43

Putting him first (5:1-15)   51

Truth – will the real God please stand up? (6:1-7:16)   58

Getting to know all about him (8:1-14)   67

Speaking the truth (9:1-10:15)   74

Bigger than all of us (11:1-11)   87

None of this (12:1-14:3)   97

A happy ending (14:4-9)   107

Some of the words in the text are printed in darker letters. This means that they come from the Bible itself.

Doing what you're told
(1:1-2:1)

GO AND GET MARRIED STOP YOUR WIFE WILL BE
UNFAITHFUL STOP AND YOUR CHILDREN WILL BE
JUST LIKE HER STOP   (1:2)

This was God's engagement-day telegram to Hosea,
his man in Israel. It was God's way of telling him to
pop the question to Gomer, one of the local glamour
girls. Not the most cheerful of greetings, you might
think. It's certainly not on a par with today's
wedding wishes of **CONGRATULATIONS, MAY
ALL YOUR TROUBLES BE LITTLE ONES.**
God's greeting read exactly the opposite. Hosea
could expect only giant-sized problems.

It's all hearts and flowers for the normal husband-
to-be. His picture-book bride floats up the aisle
towards him to the strains of the wedding march. The
stars in his eyes tend to eclipse any fears that may
lurk in the back of his mind. Things like wife swop-
ping, adultery and divorce are hidden behind a star-
spangled blindfold of love. But for Hosea, there was
no such blindfold. He proposed with his eyes wide
open. He knew there would be problems. He foresaw
one domestic tragedy after another. The only stars in
his eyes were falling ones.

'But wait a minute,' you may cry. 'Hosea was
God's faithful friend. Wasn't God asking a lot of
him? After all, he knew that Gomer would turn out
to be a bad lot. Yet he asked Hosea to marry her.'

7

The answer comes in a postscript to the telegram.

MY PEOPLE HAVE LEFT ME AND BECOME UN-
FAITHFUL STOP   (1 :2)

When we fill in the stops in that telegram, we find
that God was saying: 'Hosea, I need your help. I have
marriage problems too. Israel is my bride but she is
unfaithful. She always has been. Yet I have remained
faithful to her. I have supported her, even when she
has had love affairs with other gods. But the world
has forgotten this. Your marriage can remind them. I
want you to love Gomer and to marry her, just as I
have loved and married Israel. Gomer will have love
affairs with other men but I want you to stick by her.
This will be a picture of my marriage to Israel.'

God was going in for visual aids. He could use
Hosea's marriage as a picture. It would teach his
own bride just how unfaithful she had been to him.
Hosea was to be the loving, caring husband while
Gomer was to spend her life jumping into her
neighbours' beds.

It was no cold, calculating God who planned to use
Hosea and Gomer in this way. It was a God who
cared. He wanted to save his bride and he had tried
everything else. At first, he had given Israel a
wedding present of two precious stones. They were
inscribed with Ten Commandments.

'Stick by these,' he had said, 'and we will live
happily ever after.' Obedience was the golden rule in
this great love affair.

However, before long every one of the marriage
rules had been shattered. Next, God took a tougher
line to save his bride. He left her to her own ends.

Maybe her own mistakes would bring her to her senses. But that failed too.

Playgirl Israel was heading for a sticky end. She had failed to learn her lesson. So God decided to use a new teaching method. He chose Hosea and Gomer to act out his lesson. It was his last hope, short of turning Israel into an obedient robot. And who wants a robot for a bride?

THE MARRIAGE – DOOMED BEFORE IT STARTED

So Hosea married . . . Gomer, the daughter of Diblaim. (1:3)

Hosea was an action man. When God commanded, he acted. He knew the first rule of loving God: 'Do as you're told.' He might once have dreamed of a cosy family life in a modest semi-detached with a loving wife in the kitchen. His hopes might have included an average family-size camel in the garden shed, and probably a gaggle of kids to complete a scene of domestic bliss. But God had other ideas. And that was good enough for Hosea.

The wedding day arrived and Gomer waltzed up the aisle on daddy Diblaim's arm. Hosea's mates looked on with envy, but not the brood of sisters, cousins and aunts. They shook their heads to a tut-tut rhythm. They knew their women, and their wise old eyes could see through Gomer as though she was made of glass. Instinct told them that she would give their boy little happiness.

His hopes might have included an average family-size came

Despite this, it was a jolly affair. It might have been a 'shot-gun' wedding for Hosea, but at least he wanted his bride. In fact, he was head-over-heels in love with Gomer. It was a strong love too. In fact, it was just like the never-say-die love which God continued to shower on his bride.

The honeymoon began. They loved. They delighted in discovering each other. Later, their first child arrived. It was a boy! They settled to a comfortable family life. Hosea's engagement-day telegram was only a memory in this early contentment.

Then something happened. Not suddenly. It was gradual coldness creeping into the relationship. Once Gomer had been warm and sunny. Now the ice-age was dawning. Could this be it? Could this be the start of Gomer's adultery? It all fitted. The reluctance to meet his eyes. The unexplained absence.

The endless excuses to put off loving-making. Hosea's suspicions snowballed. But it was not until the arrival of the second child that his fears turned into reality. It was not his! 'It was the child of a shameless prostitute,' Hosea tells us in 2:4.

It was make-your-mind-up time for Hosea. He could throw his cheating wife into a pit and have his neighbours stone her to death. That was the usual punishment for adultery. Or he could forgive and try to forget.

Hosea chose to forgive. His love was too strong to be broken by Gomer's weakness for the opposite sex. And he had to consider God's plan for his marriage too. After all, it was supposed to show the world what was happening in the bigger partnership between God and Israel. In that marriage the husband was eager to forgive. It was quite amazing. Without a forgiving husband, Israel would have been battered out of existence long before Hosea came on the scene.

So Hosea and Gomer made up. The new baby, a girl, became one of the family, and life in the Hosea household settled back to normal. But it turned out to be the calm before the stormy break-up. Gomer found life dull with a serious young prophet so she took another lover – and produced yet another baby.

It was too much! In a fury, Hosea stripped Gomer of all that he had given to her. He told her to pack her belongings and leave. Had he had enough at last? At first reading it seems as though he had. God had one idea for his marriage but now the prophet seems to have another. But that is just not true. Hosea is still under God's orders. He is still doing as he is told. The marriage bust-up was all in God's plans. He wanted to show his own bride

something. If she kept on flirting with other gods
she too would be thrown out of her promised
homeland. She would be left beaten, unloved and
disowned.

In fact, this grim warning was spelt out clearly in
the names Hosea gave to his wife's three children.

THE FAMILY – WHAT'S IN A NAME?

Names are no game. Names meant serious business
to the Israelites, just as they do today. There was a
television star who warned: 'You can write what you
like about me, but spell my name wrong and I'll have
your guts for garters.' Names tell a tale. Take for
example the town of Oswaldtwistle, in the north of
England. It has long been a favourite with the
television comic. But it was serious for a certain king
called Oswald. The boundary of his kingdom ran
through this little town. If I tell you that 'twistle'
means boundary in the local dialect, you can work
the rest out for yourself. And what about Rams-
bottom over the next hill? Now before your imagination starts to run away with you, let me explain
that it is simply the valley bottom where rams used to
graze.

Names were made to work even harder in Hosea's
day. You will get the idea if I tell you that Hosea's
own name means 'salvation'. It was quite apt really.
God had chosen him for a special purpose. Hosea
had to tell Israel how she could be saved. The same
was true of Gomer's children. Their names were used
to spell out God's message.

Name him 'Jezreel', because it will not be long before I punish the king of Israel for the murders that his ancestor Jehu committed at Jezreel. (1:4)

The city of Jezreel had a bad name. It was the site of a great massacre – the place where Israel's royal family lost their crowns and their heads. The nation had been unfaithful again. It had begun to worship foreign gods and the king had encouraged this. So God stepped in. He chose someone to kill the king. His royal assassin was Jehu, a five star general. But Jehu went too far. He lopped off more heads than he should have done. He waded to the throne not only through blue blood, but also through the blood of the massacred Prime Minister and his Cabinet. But Jehu was inconsistent. In one way, he stopped too soon with his bloody coup. He ignored the pagan god problem and allowed their shrines to stay in business.

In God's eyes, Jezreel stood for all that was rotten in Israel, his marriage partner. It was a constant reminder. The earthly kings had turned their backs on him. They had gone their own way and done what they wanted.

And Jezreel also spoke volumes about Israel's love affairs with other gods. So God declared: **'I am going to put an end to Jehu's dynasty. And in the Valley of Jezreel I will at that time destroy Israel's military power.' (1:4, 5)**

Name her 'Unloved', because I will no longer show love to the people of Israel or forgive them. (1:6)

Marriage is an affair of patience. Everyone has flaws. Marriage partners are no exception. Good husbands and wives will see faults in their partners but will quickly learn to put up with them.

When it comes to patience, no one can beat God. He is perfect patience. But even that can be stretched to snapping point. Israel's day of mercy was in its last minutes, and destruction would come at the stroke of midnight.

Things looked black. Had God really abandoned his people? It seemed so. But then we read, **But to the people of Judah I will show love. I, the Lord their God, will save them. (1:7)**

God still cared. If Israel had rejected him, he would turn to Judah. She was part of his chosen people too. Like Israel, she had her faults. God knew she was not perfect. But he needed her. He had a plan to save the human race, and Judah was needed to play a vital role in it. Israel might be the older sister. She was the more powerful nation but she had let God down. Now he turned to her little sister. He would look at Judah.

CHILD NO. 3

Name him 'Not-My-People', because the people of Israel are not my people, and I am not their God. (1:9)

Now Israel had no right to God's love. She had
fallen for pagan gods. How could she claim that God
was her husband? After all, she had rarely acted the
faithful wife. In fact, ever since their marriage on
Mount Sinai, she had neglected him. Israel's life
story should have read like a promotion pamphlet
for God's kingdom. Instead it read like the diary of
an international playgirl.

THE PROMISE – HOPE FOR THE FUTURE

God had a dream. He wanted to win the human race
back to himself. The world was lost and wandering
in circles. God's marriage to Israel would be a sign-
post for men. It would say: 'Go Israel's way for
salvation.' But the bride turned the sign round. She
became as bad as the world she was supposed to
convert. She forgot God and ran after pagan gods.
Now God had decided that enough was enough.
Israel was to be rejected like an old bent coin from a
slot machine.

The bride's ugly past had caught up with her at
last. The verdict seems to be: No future. The
situation looks hopeless. But then Hosea gets a new
message coming through on his hot-line from heaven:
**The people of Israel will become like the sand of the
sea, more than can be counted or measured. Now God
says to them, 'You are not my people,' but the day is
coming when he will say to them, 'You are the children
of the living God!' (1:10)**

Somehow, the rejected, bent Israel will be ham-
mered back into shape. Just how God is going to do
this, Hosea is not saying – at least, not yet. Like any

good story-teller, he tickles his reader's curiosity and leads him on. At first he shows him the husband. He's so patient. His bride has been unfaithful for centuries. She has broken her marriage vows at every opportunity. Yet the husband has stayed loyal. He will never break his word. When God first chose Israel for his bride, he made her a promise. She would have lots of children. In fact, they would be as numerous as the grains of sand on the seashore. And God is not one to break his promise. Hosea adds: **The people of Judah and the people of Israel will be reunited. They will choose for themselves a single leader, and once again they will grow and prosper ... Yes, the day of Jezreel will be a great day! (1:11)**

Jezreel might be a black day for the people of Israel. It meant defeat. Their king and army had been destroyed. All was dust and despair. But all was not lost. New life and hope could spring out of the battle ashes. Once again the Israelites would become **God's people** and **Loved by the Lord. (2:1)**

Hope for Israel. But what about Gomer? We left her homeless and hopeless. She had been thrown out to walk the streets. The first act of the Hosea marriage drama has ended in tragedy. But stay in your seats. The curtain is about to rise on Act Two.

Trusting him
with your life
(2:2-17)

Gomer hurried along the yellow dusty streets of her home town. She was frightened. Hosea had sent her packing and now the whole neighbourhood knew of her latest escapade. Every street corner threatened danger. If it wasn't somebody trying to buy her body, it was a self-righteous gang just itching to use her for target practice.

At first, she had strode past them in defiance. If Hosea did not want her, she knew who did. Strutting through the town, she thumbed through her little black address book, and thought: **I will go to my lovers – they give me food and water, wool and linen, olive-oil and wine. (2:5)**

But Gomer had counted her lovers before they were trapped. One by one they went missing. **She will run after her lovers but will not catch them. She will look for them but will not find them (2:7).** The grapevine had travelled faster than Gomer. Her lovers had had their fun. Now they had no desire to pay the price she was asking. Surprise! Surprise! They suddenly found they had business out of town.

But the rest of the people had business in town. Gomer was *their* business. Her brazen game of hide-and-seek with her lovers had not exactly won her friends. So she decided to make herself scarce while there was still a chance. She must have time to think – time to plan her next move.

We cannot know for certain what Gomer did next. Hosea does not go into such details. But we do know something about the times. That throws some light on the situation. For instance, we know that her options were painfully few. Women's Lib was less than a twinkle in the eye of the odd woman here and there. This was the 8th Century BC. It was an age when men treated their womenfolk on the same level as the family camel. If anything, the camel was more valuable! Without a man in this man's world, Gomer knew that her survival was in question.

Her first option was to return home and plead for yet another chance. But the very thought gave her claustrophobia. She wanted freedom. She did not want to be hemmed in with religious Hosea and three brats. They were a nuisance. She hadn't even wanted the last two. No, she wanted the good things of life, and she could not trust her husband to provide those. In fact she could not trust him for anything. In that respect, she was just like God's bride. We shall soon see how.

She wanted freedom . . . the good things in life.

She did have a second choice. She could bide her time. The town's temper would soon cool. Then she could come back. She might even look for a job as a servant. Even before the idea was fully formed, she dismissed it. It was too much. After all, she had been mistress in her own house. She could never be a kitchen maid. She would be a riches to rags joke for years to come.

But the third choice was much more attractive. She could become a sacred prostitute at the local pagan temple. It would certainly give her a comfortable living. And for another thing, it would be one-in-the-eye for that pompous husband of hers. How often she had heard him ranting on about Israel's sex orgies with the pagan god, Baal! What was it he claimed his God had told him . . . ? **Israel would never acknowledge that I am the one who gave her the corn, the wine, the olive-oil, and all the silver and gold that she used in the worship of Baal. (2:8)** Yes, that was it! She had heard that sermon so many times she could preach it herself. What was the punch-line again? **I will punish her for the times that she forgot me when she burnt incense to Baal and put on her jewellery to go chasing after her lovers. (2:13)**

THE ROAD TO BAAL

Gomer knew the story well. It had all started on the day God had exchanged vows with his bride. He had just saved her from the clutches of Egypt. He had promised to love, comfort, honour and keep her. In return, the bride had vowed to love, cherish and to obey. They spent their honeymoon touring in the

Wilderness. Later, God carried his bride across the threshold of the River Jordan and into Canaan. That was to be her home. He had always promised that she would live in a country like that.

But even before the bride settled in, she began flirting with the local playboy god called Baal. She saw him as the big-spender type. He could provide all the needs of his worshippers.

Baal came along at just the right time. Israel was beginning to have second thoughts about her husband. Oh, he might have worked wonders during the desert honeymoon. He was certainly a good breadwinner. The daily delivery of manna bread had proved that. But how would he measure up to the new situation in Canaan? It was a whole new life-style. Previously, wandering Israel had thought the ground was made for walking on. Now she had to dig it – or die! She was as much at home down on the farm as a burly Liverpool docker picking daisies. Israel was as out of place as that in Canaan.

Israel's husband could conjure up bread, but could he be trusted to produce a thousand fields of corn? And what about the hundreds of vegetable patches, not to mention the many vineyards that would be needed to keep hunger and thirst at bay? Her very life was at stake. Could her husband be trusted with it?

BEWITCHED BY BAAL

Israel's husband was suspect. He might not be able to provide for her. On the the other hand, Baal seemed quite the bright boy for the new situation. The conquered Canaanites seemed to be on a winner with him. He had already proved himself. The land overflowed with good food. No kitchen pantry need be empty. There was plenty for everyone. Israel was tempted to walk out on her husband there and then and throw in her lot with Baal. However, she decided to play it smart. She kept God as her husband and made Baal her lover.

Today, man plays the same god game. We call it the Religious Insurance Game. The modern version goes something like this: You put your money on God for Sundays, weddings and funerals. After all, they are his speciality. But when it comes to the colour television or a new car for the wife, you bank on the god of materialism.

Israel's version concerned more basic things. She kept her husband safely in the background and tried to keep him happy with a few prayers and sacrifices. But when it came to the bread-and-butter issues of daily living, she ran to her lover, Baal.

For example, take the problem of rain. This was Israel's most vital need. In her new sun-blistered homeland, a long hot summer could last for years. If anyone promised rain, he was a favourite at once. Baal claimed to do just that. Israel fell for it. It was as tempting as a crate of Pepsi in the middle of the Sahara Desert.

The Canaanites used powers of suggestion to encourage Baal. Voodoo witchdoctors do the same today. They jab pins in small dummies. They think that they will kill their enemies in that way. But the Canaanites were more interested in life. They wanted

21

It was as tempting as a crate of Pepsi in the middle of the Sahara Desert.

it to go on and be renewed. And they did not go in for the doll idea either. They had a much more enjoyable method. They wanted to encourage new life in Mother Earth. If they produced new life in the wombs of sacred prostitutes, surely Baal would get the message? You could say that the cult's motto was: 'A prostitute a day keeps the drought at bay.'

Now you might think that this was just a great excuse for sex on demand. And you would be right for some of Baal's worshippers. But the majority were hooked on this pagan superstition. It was so potent that Israel soon became addicted.

Well, that was the story. That was how Hosea had told it so often. To Gomer, it was all a giggle, the more so because it angered her husband so much.

'Oh to be a Baal prostitute,' she thought. 'Sweet revenge!' However, there was one obstacle. She had to go before the Baal Temple selection committee. Three children had not exactly improved her vital statistics, and the Baal priests were known to be choosy over new recruits. Her chances, unlike her figure, were slim.

That left the fourth option. Gomer could set herself up in opposition to the temple ladies. She was sure she could undercut their fancy prices. Already she had discovered there were plenty of street-corner customers. It was the last alternative. There was no other choice. She only had to wait for tempers to cool. Then she could return, rent a room off a back alley and go into the business of selling herself.

A never-say-die affair
(2:2-17)

Meanwhile, back in the Hosea household, life was about as cheerful as a waiting room in a maternity hospital. Time had dragged by. It had been so frustrating. Hosea had paced every inch of his one-up, one-down home. The waiting seemed endless. He had spent a lifetime at it or so it seemed. His beloved Gomer was in a back-street brothel and he wanted so much to rescue her. But he waited.

He waited because he was under God's orders. He had to keep on reminding himself that his domestic life was not just his own affair. It was on show to the nation. God had served a separation order on Israel, and in his turn Hosea had given Gomer notice to quit. The lesson was there for the learning. Israel had to watch out. Unless she stopped playing around with her lover, she would share Gomer's fate. She would be stripped of everything and thrown out of her homeland.

God's words to his bride were, **'She would never acknowledge that I am the one who gave her the corn, the wine, the olive-oil, and all the silver and gold that she used in the worship of Baal. So at harvest time I will take back my gifts . . . I will strip her naked in front of her lovers, and no one will be able to save her from my power. I will put an end to all her festivities . . . all her religious meetings. I will punish her for the times that she forgot me.'** (2:8-13)

So Hosea waited – and suffered. Gomer and her

brothel often made the headlines on the daily grapevine. Each newsy tit-bit packed a sickening punch. Yet Hosea's private little hell was often the doorway into heaven itself. The more he was hurt, the more he searched for God. And as he drew nearer to God, he began to see amazing things.

For one thing, Hosea saw that God's situation was far worse than anything he had ever experienced himself. His own heartbreak was measured in years, but God's torment over his bride spanned centuries. For another thing, Hosea was spared a clinch-by-clinch view of Gomer's ugly affairs. But not God. He had to endure each sordid act of his bride's adultery every minute of every day of every year.

And yet, amazingly, God still wanted his bride back. His love was just not human. It was never-ending. It was a never-say-die love. It was a love that Hosea was learning to have towards his own bride. And the more he learnt it, the shorter grew the waiting time. God was preparing him for the next stage in the marriage drama.

Soon the waiting would end. Hosea would win back Gomer, just as God would one day woo back Israel. But how was this to be achieved? That was the question. The answer came in two parts. First, there was the easy, kid-glove approach. Then, if that failed, came the hard iron fist.

THE EASY WAY

My children, plead with your mother — though she is no longer a wife to me, and I am no longer her husband. Plead with her to stop her adultery and prostitution. (2:2)

Hosea tried this way first, and God did too. He would rather whisper to Israel than slap her. And like Hosea, he chose his messengers carefully. He sent the faithful children of his marriage with Israel. They were loyal to him, just as Hosea's children stood by him. They could carry his words of warning. And so he calls to them: 'My children, go and plead with your motherland . . .'

Hosea might have done the same thing. He might have collected his children and sent them to Gomer. Imagine the scene. The children run off, eager to bring their mummy home. One moment their eyes are alight with hope, the next they are darkened by tears. They had caught her between lovers. They began to plead . . . she laughed . . . called them fools . . . then slammed the door in their faces.

In fact this is precisely what happened to God when his children pleaded with Israel. Whenever people like Hosea urged their motherland to give up her false lovers, they were treated like fools. They were either laughed out of town – or thrown out.

It was clear that Israel would never heed a softly whispered warning. It was now time to throw away the kid gloves. If Israel was to survive, God had to get tough. It was the only hope.

THE HARD WAY

I am going to take her into the desert again; there I will win her back with words of love. I will . . . make Trouble Valley a door of hope.   (2:14, 15)

There was only one way Gomer and Israel would now learn their lessons. They had to go the hard way,

They began to plead . . . she laughed . . . then slammed the door.

through Trouble Valley. Both Gomer and Israel were to fall on difficult times. Then they would gladly turn back to their husbands for help. Today, we have a wise saying: 'Only when you're flat on your back do you look up to God.' Its message is clear. Trouble Valley will be a door of hope.

700 years after Hosea's time, Jesus was to sum up his truth in the story of the Prodigal Son. The young son is fed up with farm life. He throws it in and heads for the city and the bright lights. But soon the money runs out and he ends up a penniless labourer in a

pigsty. Then he comes to his senses. He stop
wallowing in a self-made trough of troubles an
cries out: 'What a fool I've been. I will go back to m
Father and beg his forgiveness.' (Luke 15:11f)

Trouble was going to come for Gomer and Israel
They would lose everything they held dear – money
treasures, festivities, food and home. They would
even lose their freedom, and finish in slavery. Only
then would they cry out: **'I am going back to my firs**
husband – I was better off then than I am now.'   (2:7

Trouble is bubbling up for both brides. In the cas
of Gomer it is nearly upon her. Soon, she would no
longer be selling herself. Somebody would be sellin
her! Gomer was about to descend into her Troubl
Valley. But it would prove to be the doorway to hope

Taking her back
(2:18-3:5)

Gomer was at the end of her tether – a slave's tether, to be precise. She was chained by the neck in the local slave market; a piece of human flesh for sale. This was her valley of trouble. She had to tumble to the very bottom before she found the way out.

Hope came in the form of Hosea. He stood in the middle of the haggling market crowd. In one hand he had a small cash bag; by his side, a couple of sacks of barley. He was obviously in the market for something . . . or somebody. Could it possibly be for her?

Gomer need not have worried. God knew that she had learnt her lesson at last. He knew how she felt. She was really sorry that she had left Hosea. And that was all he wanted to know. When Hosea tuned in to God that morning, he received the following message: **'Go again and show your love for a woman who is committing adultery . . . You must love her just as I still love the people of Israel.'** (3:1) There was no need for names. Hosea knew very well which woman God had in mind, and he also understood her hopeless situation. For years he had looked on with a sad kind of loving. He had watched life do an about-turn and kick Gomer the gaiety girl into the gutter. Now he could go to her rescue.

So God's man set off for market that morning to bid for Gomer. He took with him **fifteen pieces of silver and 150 kilograms of barley to buy her.** (3:2) In all, it would barely have kept a large family fed for a month. It added up to half the going rate for a normal female slave. She was a knock-down lot, fit only for the bargain counter.

Slave day was gossip day, and everyone knew it. People came from far and near to look at the slaves and to listen to the talk. And today, they talked about Gomer. They had been talking about her for weeks. It was such a scandal. She'd really come down in the world. But this week their eyes lit up and their tongues wagged faster. Gomer's story became a headline sensation. Hosea was trying to buy her. The

The holy man had opened the bidding for this out of work prostitute.

holy man had opened the bidding for this out of work prostitute. Within minutes, it was the talk of the town as tongues tripped into top gear:

'I'd rather be dead than bid for that slut . . .'

'He must be out of his mind, after what she's done to him . . .'

'She should be stoned, not sold . . .'

Going . . . Going . . . GONE to Hosea. The

hammer fell. She was his again. The neighbours gaped in amazement. But Hosea took no notice. He shouldered his way past and set off with Gomer in tow. They walked away together, once again man and wife. This was the astonishing punch-line to the marriage drama. And God used that unexpected twist in the tale. It was his message of hope for his own bride. 'Israel, I will make you my wife . . . I will keep my promise and make you mine, and you will acknowledge me as Lord.' (2:19, 20) Oh yes, God would still give Israel her marching orders, just as Hosea had done with Gomer. One day, Israel would also be a slave. She would be sold to foreigners. But then he would step in. Soon the time would be right. God would rescue his bride – and this time there would be no mistake. Then he would say, 'You are my people,' and they will answer, 'You are our God.' (2:23)

Meanwhile, Hosea and Gomer walked home. They left an astonished crowd behind them. The whole town was flabbergasted. It was unbelievable. How could Hosea lower himself? How could he take her back? She was just not worth it. She was only a woman after all. Still, perhaps he planned to punish her. If your dog misbehaves, you beat it. Gomer was only Hosea's wife. She must really be in for a thrashing. And she deserved it. The crowd waited expectantly. But they were to be disappointed.

Gomer had suffered enough. Hosea knew that life had already beaten her into submission. There was no need to hammer home the lesson with a big stick. But Hosea knew something else too. Gomer was a person not a possession. She was his beloved wife not

31

a disobedient animal. And so, Hosea took his wife back home, and the cheated crowd shuffled back to the fun of the slave fair.

In the growing stillness, the couple faced one another – and their future. What to do? What do you say in a situation like this? How can you piece together a relationship? Gomer had a lot to learn. Her marriage to Hosea had been torn to shreds. A thousand cutting remarks had slashed it about. Hundreds of sharp actions had damaged it. Now Gomer knew that she must say 'Sorry'. And that was only the first lesson. If the couple wanted a happy marriage, a second lesson was needed.

THE LESSON OF LOVE

To Gomer, love was a physical, four letter word, and probably a dirty one after all she had been through. Love was being pawed by any one who could pay the right price. Love was using your body to meet the cost of living. Love was sex spelt another way!

But Hosea knew differently. Sex was only an act of love. It was not love itself. It was a physical sign. Through sex, people could express a deeper truth. It could show that they loved one another. If sex was used rightly, it could give delight. After all, it had this special meaning. If only Gomer knew this. How could Hosea teach her? As he watched his bride, he came to a decision: **I told her that for a long time she would have to wait for me without being a prostitute or committing adultery; and during this time I would wait for her. (3:3)**

A ban on sex! It was the only answer. Gomer had

lived for sex. When she had a relationship with a man, it was a sexual one. She did not know any other sort. If you took that away from her, she would have to think again. She would have to find what love and marriage were all about.

'And God's bride will have to learn that lesson too,' says Hosea. And she would learn it in the same way . . . **Israel will have to live for a long time without kings or leaders, without sacrifices or sacred stone pillars, without idols or images. (3:4)** Like Gomer, Israel was hooked on the physical side of her relationship with her husband and lovers. She showed her love through physical objects. She surrounded herself with leaders, sacrifices and religious trappings. She gave these things to God but she kept her soul. She used the religious objects just as Gomer had used sex. When Gomer needed groceries, she sold her body. When Israel needed God's provisions, she sacrificed to Baal. While Gomer found warmth by snuggling into the embraces of men, Israel found comfort by wrapping herself round with strong leaders and soothing religious rites. Israel and Gomer were two of a pair. They wanted love without having to love. 'Get' not 'give' was their motto and they tried to get as much as possible.

And so God warned Israel. She gave so little. Now she would lose what she already had. God would take away her religious trappings. They symbolized Israel's relationship to him. She would be stripped of everything. She would be led away from her temples, shrines and idols. She would be forced to think. She would have to ask herself questions. What was her marriage to God all about? What did it mean to love him?

THE GIFTS OF LOVE

But this is not God's last word. Hosea's story had a happy twist. And that gave Israel a long-term hope.

But the time will come when the people of Israel will once again turn to the Lord their God ... Then they will fear the Lord and receive his good gifts. (3:5)

'Good gifts' is probably the greatest understatement in Hosea's book. God's gift list adds up to nothing less than Paradise! Just run your eyes down the list of God's presents to his bride:

I will make a covenant with all the wild animals ... so that they will not harm my people. I will also remove all weapons of war ... I will let my people live in peace and safety.

> **I will make you my wife;**
> **I will be true and faithful; ...**
> **I will answer the prayers of my people Israel.**
> **I will make rain fall on the earth,**
> **and the earth will produce corn and**
> **grapes and olives.**
> **I will establish my people in the land**
> **and make them prosper.**
> **I will show love ...**
> **I will say, 'You are my people.' (2:18-23)**

When God made his marriage vows to Israel and said, 'I will,' he was not pretending. He promised his bride heaven! Israel will certainly have to descend into Trouble Valley, but one day she will climb out into a land of peace.

In today's terms, it will be a world without a bloody Ulster, without a starving Bangladesh, with no mushroom bomb, with no criminals. All the police forces could lay up their truncheons. It will be a world in which you will not only be able to pat your pet dog, but also cuddle a lion or even a gorilla, if the fancy takes you. There will be perfect harmony in creation. All creatures will love others as they would wish to be loved. God's bride will return his love and they will live happily ever after.

. . . cuddle . . . a gorilla.

And so, God's bride is heading for heaven, eventually. As for Hosea's bride, there was to be no such fairy-tale ending for her, at least not on this earth. She was still learning in the school of love. She was busy picking up the pieces of a shattered home life.

Letting justice be done
(4:1-19)

Home might have been a headache to Gomer, but she could cope. She had had a narrow escape. Slavery was an awful fate. It was like a living death. Compared to that, home was heaven. She could learn to get alongside her now grown-up children. She could adjust to life with a man of God. She could even learn to live with the local busybodies who treated her like a bad smell. In fact, she had much for which she could be thankful. So too had Hosea.

Family life was probably almost as good as that first honeymoon year minus the cuddles. This minus left Gomer a little bewildered. She still had a lot to learn about love. The minus also affected Hosea. He was left with a patient kind of longing. He might be God's man, but he was also Gomer's very human husband. No doubt he longed to do what comes naturally to man and wife. He wanted this closeness just as God desired a deep intimacy between himself and his bride. But for the sake of love, Hosea's relationship had to be an arm's length affair, just as it would one day have to be between God and Israel.

So Gomer struggled on in the elementary school of love. Meanwhile, her husband was receiving a much more comprehensive education in the shady love life of God's bride. God taught him: **'There is no faithfulness or love in the land, and the people do not acknowledge me as God.'** (4:1)

Israel refused to accept God as her one, true husband.

She had not only broken all her marriage vows, she had also spent her wedding anniversaries making eyes at other gods. This divine love story has now ended up in court. Charges have been levelled against the unfaithful bride.

BREACH OF PROMISE

The bride has been charged with breach of promise before the High Court of Heaven. **The Lord has an accusation to bring against the people.** **(4:1)** Soon the trial is over and the verdict given. Israel is guilty. Now Hosea is summoned. He is the court's messenger and he has a job to do. The Lord Chief Justice wants him to deliver the sentence. Hosea has to tell guilty Israel about her punishment.

He is the ideal man for the job. He has been trained for this very moment. *His* marriage has been unhappy too. He has loved his wife and been separated from her. In a way, he has seen and understood God's love and anger towards Israel. Now he can go to God's unfaithful bride. He can speak with understanding. He is ready. His message is ready. The messenger is sent.

THE COURT'S MESSAGE

Hosea's first speech was probably to a home-town audience. And that must have taken all his courage. When he last stood before them he was bidding for a down-and-out prostitute. This time he came to bid for their attention. He carried the charge and verdict of God's High Court.

Picture the scene. Quickly he strides across the bustling market place and stands on the very stage to which Gomer had been tethered:

'Quiet!' he thunders. **'The Lord has an accusation to bring against the people who live in this land.'** An embarrassed hush descends on the jostling crowd. The merry market chatter dwindles to curious whispers. **Listen, Israel, to what he says, 'There is no faithfulness or love . . . The people do not acknowledge me as God. They make promises and break them; they lie, murder, steal, and commit adultery.'** (4:1, 2)

Our modern permissive society is not new. Israel had the same set of problems 2,700 years ago. Suppose you stood up in your home town market and shouted the same words. Just imagine the reaction. People would laugh; they'd heckle; they'd shout, 'Mind your own business!' A permissive society allows lots of things but it will not permit criticism. It cannot afford it, and Israel certainly could not afford Hosea.

'Who does he think he is . . . ?'

'What on earth's he fussing about . . . ?'

'We've enough to worry about . . .'

And that gives Hosea a cue. The people moan and groan so God will give them a reason. There will be a drought and their evil will have caused it. **And so the land will dry up, and everything that lives on it will die.** (4:3) This quick-fire reply gags the rumbling crowd. Drought is always headline news, and no one wants to miss any ideas about it.

Hosea's words add up to this: 'Listen, Israel. You've run out on your husband once too often. You've thanked your lover, Baal, for providing corn

Who does he think he is?

and wine. But your real husband is the true bread-winner. Now he is going to withhold his provisions. He will not provide the rain for your crops any more. You will just have a long hot summer.'

CROOKS IN PRIESTS' CLOTHING

The local priests know what Hosea is getting at. He is about to give their profitable little game away. They cannot allow that to happen. They begin to heckle, but Hosea makes them wish they had stayed at home with their sacred prostitutes. **The Lord says, 'Let no one accuse the people . . . my complaint is against you priests. Night and day you blunder on . . . You priests have refused to acknowledge me and have rejected my teaching, and so I reject you . . . The more of you priests there are, the more you sin against me . . . You grow rich from the sins of my people, and so you want them to sin more and more.' (4:4-8)**

The priests' business was supposed to be pious religion but they had turned it into a protection racket. They were the Al Capones of Hosea's day and the Roaring Twenties scene was just a whisper in comparison. Their slogan was, 'Sin now, pay later.' The people could sin as much as they liked today. Tomorrow they had to bring animal sacrifices to the temple.

Not any old bull or cow would do. It had to be perfect. Of course, the shrewd priests were quick to corner the cattle market. They judged that only their own cattle were good enough. They could not lose. One moment they sold a cow for a fat profit and the next moment the buyer was handing it back to them free of charge!

But the priests did not stop there. They actually wanted their people to sin more. So they encouraged them. They really practised what they preached. They mugged and murdered pilgrims en route to the Baal temples. No one escaped. If the ambush squads didn't relieve them of their money, the cattle men did. It was just one big confidence trick.

By the time Hosea had finished, the crooked priests hadn't a leg to stand on. Their job was clear enough. They had to teach Israel the facts of life. She was married to God. She was supposed to be faithful to her husband and his commands. The priests knew this and they knew that they had to encourage Israel. Instead, they did exactly the opposite. They threw away the Ten Marriage Commandments, mixed God up with Baal and added a few prostitutes. That would keep the people interested.

Now God tells Israel, 'Enough is enough. The priests and people are going to learn a hard lesson.

They will find out that crime does not pay! I will punish you and make you pay for the evil you do!' (4:9)

WHO ARE YOU CALLING A FOOL?

Hosea stands before his neighbours, pleading and threatening. But he has about as much effect as today's sea-side sandwich board man. He shouts, 'Prepare to meet thy doom!' and the crowd just laugh and call him a fool. But Hosea is sharp-witted. Quick as inspiration, he turns the jibe back on the people. The Lord says, 'Wine . . . is robbing my people of their senses. They ask for revelations from a piece of wood!' (4:11-12)

Hosea cries, 'You call me a fool. What about yourselves? You chop down a tree, use some of it for firewood and carve the rest into a fancy image. Then you fall down to worship it. You talk to the trees, but they don't listen to you. They can neither hear nor help you.'

Hosea drives home his point. He quotes an old Israelite proverb: 'A people without sense will be ruined' . . . The people of Israel are under the spell of idols . . . After drinking much wine, they delight in their prostitution. (4:14-18)

JUDAH BEWARE!

Hosea gets carried away. Israel has her faults but so has her sister state. In the middle of his outburst he changes his tune. He warns Judah as well. 'Even though you people of Israel are unfaithful to me, may Judah not be guilty of the same thing. (4:15)

God has a message for Judah. He goes on, 'Don't follow in your sister's footsteps. Don't be a stubborn ass like Israel. Let your master lead you into green pastures. Come to me, Judah. My valley is green and peaceful. The false gods cannot match it.'

Hosea must have felt as if he was talking to a stone wall. Only echoes came back. The market crowd mimicked his words of warning. So he walked away. As he left, he flung God's warning over his shoulder: the people **will be carried away as by the wind, and they will be ashamed of their pagan sacrifices.'** (4:19)

Knowing who's in charge
(5:1-15)

Hosea was one man against a town. Soon he must take on a whole nation. Yesterday in the market place was just a dress rehearsal. Today, he must set out to give a command performance before royalty. He is God's ambassador to Israel. He carries a high-priority message. He has orders to go right to the top with it. He must take his message to the leaders of church and state. It is quite a task. But God has given him the exact words. **'Listen to this, you priests! Pay attention, people of Israel! Listen, you that belong to the royal family! You are supposed to judge with justice – so judgement will fall on you. You have become a trap at Mizpah, a net spread on Mount Tabor, a deep pit at Acacia City.'** (5:1, 2)

Israel has become her own worst enemy. She is a death-trap to herself. She had put justice in the hands of certain men. They were supposed to uphold the law. Instead they had become a law to themselves. This did not just happen in one part of the country. It went on everywhere. From Mizpah in the north to Tabor in the south, the people were trapped. They could not escape injustice. It was as if they had tumbled into the famous bottomless pit at Acacia City.

This was a message fit for a king who had gone crooked. He had sold out to gangsters in the nation's corridors of power. Imagine the Underworld taking over England's Houses of Parliament, or the Mafia moving into the White House in Washington. There you have the corrupt picture of Israel in the 8th Century BC.

And now Hosea had to challenge these people. He was crazy! As he packed for the journey and waved goodbye, there was no certainty that he would return. He might be performing before royalty but one thing was certain. He would not get an Oscar. More likely he would end up with an assassin's knife between the shoulder blades.

It was one thing to talk to the local priests. You could always tell them some home truths. But just try it with a king, especially one who had been rigging the nation's courts.

8th century BC Israel was no democracy. Troubleshooters usually shot themselves into trouble. Israel reckoned that she had more than her share of that already. She was surrounded by a variety of ill-tempered neighbours. In the north, mighty Assyria sat growling fiercely and in the south lay menacing Egypt. Whenever these two squared up, the tiny, wedge-shaped kingdom of Israel inevitably felt the squeeze. No! Israel had enough to handle from outside pressure. She did not need an internal rebellion. Loud-mouthed prophets up from the country were not popular.

Hosea's mind juggled with these unpleasant facts as his home town shrank to a speck on the sandy horizon. But there was yet one more thought to be thrown in. Israel was rather touchy when it came to prophets of doom. The reason for this was easy to spot. While the prophets walked closely with God, Israel and her kings were often out of step with him. So men like Hosea were a nuisance. They had been getting under royal feet ever since Israel began crowning her leaders. They asked to be trampled on and usually they were. As always, might was right in the short run.

1046 AND ALL THAT

At this stage, it may help to turn a page or two of the history book. We leave the 8th Century BC and travel 300 years back in time. First we discover that God never intended Israel to have flesh and blood kings. He had made her. He had looked after her. He was the king. He wanted to keep it that way. If she ne ded earthly governors, he would give her some. He appointed judges who could run the daily affairs of state. But he was supreme monarch.

All went reasonably smoothly at first. Then a couple of the nation's lawmen turned outlaws. Their crooked behaviour caused a storm of protest. It led to an overwhelming vote of 'no confidence' in the judges' regime. The chief judge was Samuel. He was called upon to resign and hand over state affairs to a king. His position was rather delicate to say the least. For one thing, the renegade judges were his own two sons. But there was even more to it than this. His sons had merely brought matters to a head. The controversy had been raging for most of Samuel's ministry. The Israelites had a strong argument. Other nations had kings, so why not them? If anything, their need for a king was greater. They were threatened on every border. They needed a really great leader. Only such a man could rally the tribes of Israel into one fighting unit.

Samuel took the matter to God for a decision. God

told him that the decision had already been made – by
Israel! God was no dictator. His subjects had
freedom to choose their leader. However, the people
were warned that they would have to pay dearly for
de-throning God.

As Hosea's camel see-sawed across the hot desert
towards the royal city, the prophet had time to think.
He knew just what God had meant. Those first
outlaw judges had been a bad lot but look at this
king! Compared with him, the judges were almost
saints. However, Israel's royal line had gone crooked
long before Hosea's day. The first bad king was, in
fact, the first king. The royal line began with:

SAUL

He started well but later turned a deaf ear to
God's orders. He met a violent end. (1 Samuel
8-15)

Israel then fell to . . .

DAVID

Now dawned Israel's golden age. The young
giant-killer brought the nation back to God's
rule, and the Promised Land at last became a
reality. Now it was an empire in miniature.
(2 Samuel 1-24)

But soon, the royal line was once again on the wobble.
David was succeeded by his son. . .

SOLOMON

He might have been famous for his wisdom, but not his wages. He turned his subjects into navvies and made them build splendid palaces and a temple. Then he started a tax fiddle. He really bled the people. He used every dodge in his lop-sided law book and soon he had a kingdom of paupers. (1 Kings 1-12)

Solomon's death brought relief to the forced labour camps, and the inmates were more than ready to welcome his son and successor . . .

REHOBOAM

However, there were conditions. He must cut the taxes and end the chain gangs. But Rehoboam was a bit of a hot-head. He rejected the terms on his Coronation Day, and instead doubled taxes at a stroke. It was too much! The workers came out on strike and their shop steward, Jeroboam, refused to negotiate. (1 Kings 12)

The revolt ended when the nation was split in two by a . . .

GREAT REVOLT

God's warning about royalty had come true. In less than a century, everything was in ruins. Injustice, violence and tyranny reigned supreme.

The workers came out on strike.

Israel had dethroned her heavenly king. Now she was paying the real price.

ISRAEL, THE NORTHERN KINGDOM UNDER JEROBOAM

The ten most northern tribes declared UDI, and Jeroboam was promoted to the throne. The rebels called themselves Israel after the largest of the tribes.

JUDAH, THE SOUTHERN KINGDOM
UNDER REHOBOAM

But the remaining two tribes of Judah and
Benjamin stayed loyal to the true royal line.
They accepted Rehoboam as king. (1 Kings
12-14)

When it came to the great revolt, Hosea's mind
went north. It was only natural. He himself had been
born in the Northern Kingdom. A century and a half
had passed since Jeroboam and Rehoboam had
quarrelled. It was now only an exciting story. Hosea
must have heard it often as he sat listening to his
father and grandfather. It must really have captured
his imagination. After all it had all the ingredients of
a cloak-and-dagger thriller. There was a bloody
civil war, a running 100-year battle against un-
friendly neighbours, plus a palace revolt or an
assassination every so often. (2 Kings 13-17)

It probably sounded more like a fairy tale than
real life. When Hosea was a child, Israel had one of
the few calm periods of her stormy history. She
seemed a prosperous and happy nation. Hosea saw
only peace and plenty around him. But as he grew
up, he saw things differently and what he saw
sickened him. Injustice hung around the cities like
the smell of bad drains. Israel's high society piously
performed their religious rites on the Sabbath Day.
But the rest of the week was spent differently. They
trod the poor masses deeper into a mire of poverty.
You didn't have to be a prophet to see the hypocrisy
in that.

Now Hosea was ready to face the authorities who were responsible for this injustice. His journey was nearly over. Ahead lay the city, shimmering like a giant yellow jelly in the desert heat haze. He was also to find the citizens themselves all aquiver – with fright!

Putting him first
(5:1-15)

A shocked silence descended on the city crowd. If
there had been such a thing as a pin in Hosea's day,
he could have heard one drop. As it was, the only
sound to be heard was the echo of his own voice. He
had just thundered out the charge against the king:
'You are supposed to judge with justice – so judgement
will fall on you.'   (5:1)

And then came the awful silence. It was the silence
of amazement. Only madmen and people with
suicide in mind shouted such things. You might just
whisper it to your best friend but only after looking
over your shoulder first. You made sure there were
no prying ears around. Yet here was this stranger
from the outback actually blurting the accusation in
the king's face. He was either a brave man or a fool –
perhaps both!

Hosea paused for effect then carried on: 'The evil
that the people have done prevents them from re-
turning to their God. Idolatry has a powerful hold on
them ... Their sins make them stumble and fall, and the
people of Judah fall with them . . . They take
their sheep and cattle to offer as sacrifices to the Lord,
but it does them no good. They cannot find him, for he
has left them. They have been unfaithful to the Lord;
... So now they and their lands will soon be destroyed
... Raise the war cry at Bethel! The day of punishment
is coming.'   (5:4-9)

As Hosea unfolded the charge, the crowd found

their voices. A thousand protests, some verging on panic, broke about Hosea's ears. And it was understandable. After all, he was addressing the frightened remains of a once-proud Israel. The national army had recently been squashed into submission between the bulldozing forces of Assyria and Judah. The people were busy crying over their dead. They had no time to bother about war cries. They were war-weary. They longed for peace not panic. Instead they got a gloomy prophet who told them that their troubles were only just starting.

The outburst did not surprise Hosea. He had foreseen Israel's moment of defeat for at least a decade. He had seen it coming ever since Israel had ditched her husband yet again and run to her neighbours for help.

LIFE IN A HAREM

If we really want to understand Hosea, we must look at the history book again. This particular story starts some years back. A new king had come to power in Assyria. He was Tiglath Pileser III, and he was a very ambitious man. He wanted power, power and more power. He began to look around him greedily and his eyes fell on Israel. She was only a tiny state just right for a take-over bid. So Tiglath sent in his strong-arm brigade.

Poor Israel trembled. What should she do? Well, as God's bride she could run to her husband. He would protect her. He would help her. But Israel had another choice. She could crawl for mercy before Tiglath's bullies. She weighed up the two chances and made her decision. Her husband seemed to be no match for the challenge. He would not be able to cope. So Israel threw herself at Tiglath's feet and pleaded for help, and pleaded as she had done so many times before. **When Israel saw how sick she was and when Judah saw her own wounds, then Israel went to Assyria to ask the great emperor for help. (5:13)**

So Israel threw herself at Tiglath's feet.

And Tiglath obliged. He fell upon helpless Israel and raped her of honours and wealth. Then he forced her to join his harem of nations. The bride now had a new master and a new life-style. Her husband was left out in the cold.

Soon a puppet king was set over Israel, and Tiglath made sure that he himself pulled the strings. He continued to have his way with the stolen bride. Now he could enjoy her charms whenever he felt the inclination.

However, life in the harem did not suit everybody.

A certain young Israelite nationalist called Pekah had other dreams for his country. He formed the Israelite Liberation Front. His aim was to rescue Israel from Assyria's clutches. There were no Jumbo Jets to hijack in those days, so Pekah did the next best thing. He and his guerrillas took over the royal palace. Next morning, Israel's puppet king was found with his throat and strings cut. Israel also found herself with a new king – Pekah the assassin. And the new king was quick to tell Tiglath what he could do with his harem.

Now the members of the Assyrian harem were not supposed to behave like that. Apart from anything else, it was a bad example to the others. So Tiglath felt obliged to send in his troops. Once again, Israel, the bride, faced a decision. She could still have fled back to the protecting arms of her husband. Instead she ran past them and on to her next-door neighbour. This was Damascus, capital of Syria. She successfully wooed the Syrian's support, and then turned south to make eyes at Judah. This time, Israel's advances were snubbed. But Pekah was too proud to take no for an answer. He decided to teach the sulky sister state a lesson.

Now it was Judah's turn to choose. Should she go with God or find another protector? She chose the latter. Within days, she had married forces with Assyria and caught Israel in a rather nasty pincer movement. Israel scuttled back home. But she was in for a shock. There was almost no home to go to. While Israel was away from home pushing her little sister around, Tiglath had paid a visit. Now Israel was in a worse position than before. Her leaders were rounded up like sheep and herded to the other end of the Assyrian Empire. Meanwhile, Judah reigned victorious. She really rubbed it in. She even took over a large chunk of lower Israel for herself. Pekah found himself on the other end of an assassin's knife, and Israel found herself with yet another new king. This time it was Hoshea (not to be confused with our prophet). Hoshea's first royal act was to lead a sorrowful Israel back into the Assyrian harem.

Here the history book ends. We are back in the present. Now King Hoshea came face to face with the prophet Hosea. God's man had a harsh message for the king and his badly frightened subjects. They had lost one battle but it was only the first. They would lose many more and the war would ruin them.

JUDGEMENT ON JUDAH

There ·vas at least a small consolation for the Israelites. They would not go down alone. **The Lord says, 'I am angry because the leaders of Judah have invaded Israel and stolen land from her. So I will pour out punishment on them like a flood.' (5:10)**

For once Hosea had the crowd on his side. They had always said the same thing. Judah was no good. She had gone against God. After all, God himself had originally chosen where each tribe should live. Now Judah had changed the boundaries. She had almost told God to mind his own business. It was disgraceful. Israel became very self-righteous. She always knew just when to bring God into affairs of state. It had to be when it suited her, not him.

But Hosea was not going to let them get away with

it. His next words from the Lord put a stop to the eager nods of approval in the crowd: **'Israel is suffering oppression . . . because she insisted on going for help to those who had none to give. I will bring destruction on Israel and ruin on the people of Judah.'** (5:11, 12)

IDOLATRY – THE ROOT OF ALL EVIL

In these two sentences, Hosea really strikes home. He goes to the heart of the problem relationship between God and his bride. Israel rarely put her husband first. She always went to others for help. She either idolized her lover Baal, or ran to her next-door neighbours for aid. She hardly ever gave her husband a thought. Her crime was idolatry, says Hosea. This was the root cause of all her evil. **Idolatry has a powerful hold on them.** (5:4)

In Hosea's book, an idol is whatever knocks God into second place. If God is not Number One then you are worshipping an idol. You have another god. In the ancient world there were many gods. Hosea stands out against them. If he had been around today, he would still have been busy. We have just as many idols as the Egyptians and the Assyrians. There is the well-known god, 'Profit' or 'Pay Packet'. He is very popular. He comes top of the god league. The love of money is often first in people's lives.

Then there is the great god 'Ball'. Jim is one of his followers. Every Saturday afternoon he worships at the Ball Temple for 90 minutes. He chants his petitions from his terraced pew and flips through his prayer book, the official programme. His Bible is the ports paper on a Saturday and his commentaries are he daily sports pages.

Today, millions worship Ball. In Hosea's day millions bowed to Baal. Today, the nation's leaders refer to the god of Power. They ignore the real God and put all their faith in nuclear treaties and trade agreements. The leaders of Hosea's time did exactly he same.

Israel had refused to put God first. Now she was in a mess. She had ruined her life. It was all her own fault. But this was only a taste of what was to come, says Hosea. He passes the Lord's warning on to the crowd: **'I will attack the people of Israel and Judah like a lion. I myself will tear them to pieces and then leave them . . . Perhaps in their suffering they will try to find me.'** (5:14, 15)

Truth... will the real God please stand up
(6:1-7:16)

Hosea's audience must have been tempted to tear him to pieces after his last remark. Could this Hosea not see how religious they were? Wasn't the city air still heavy with the sick-sweet smell of burnt animal flesh? Why, the city had broken all records for animal sacrifices ever since the war! Surely this Hosea man was talking through his turban. No God would tear Israel to pieces after such religious fervour.

However, blindness was not one of Hosea's failings. He kept his eyes open. When he arrived he found the city's priests working like slaves. Outside the temple he had to squeeze past crowds of people and animals and the smoke from the altars mushroomed high into the sky. Hosea looked around and he understood. The people were frightened. They knew that God was angry with them and they wanted to make their peace with him. They were even praying. Hosea listened in: **'Let's return to the Lord! He has hurt us, but he will be sure to heal us ... In two or three days he will revive us ...'** (6:1-2)

While Israel's religious leaders were crying 'Revival', Hosea could only shout, 'Sham!'

PROMISES! PROMISES!

'Israel and Judah, what am I going to do with you? Your love for me disappears as quickly as morning mist.' (6:4)

These two sentences paint the whole sad picture. Israel's love was like the old jokes about the weather. If the sun was forecast, you made sure you took an umbrella. Israel's love always promised much but never delivered the goods. Hosea puts it this way: Dawn was a time of promise. With it came mist and mist meant moisture. The parched desert land of

If the sun was forecast, you made sure you took an umbrella.

Israel reached out for this. It expected more. But then the sun came up and the mist vanished in the warm air. All was dry again. Israel's love was just like that mist. When the nation was born, she loved God. She promised more love. But things got too hot and the love disappeared. Israel would quickly swop her affections to Baal or her next-door neighbours. It was only when the new loves failed that she remembered God and tried to worm her way back into his affections.

Israel's love was a lie. It was just play acting. It was a love that said sorry but never really meant it. It was a love that said one thing and then did the opposite. Israel's actions spoke louder than her sweet-nothings.

If the angels had had a popular daily newspaper in heaven at about this time, they would have read some interesting stories. Israel's unloving actions would make front page news. The headings might read:

GOD'S BRIDE
TEARS UP
WEDDING
PROMISES

The people have broken the covenant I had made with them. (6:7)

GANGLAND
TAKEOVER
BY
PRIESTS

The priests are like a gang of robbers . . . (6:9)

THE SORDID
LOVE LIFE
OF A
BRIDE

My people have defiled themselves by worshipping idols. (6:10)

THEFT AND
MUGGING
BREAK ALL
RECORDS

They cheat one another; they break into houses and steal; they rob people in the streets. (7:1)

ANARCHISTS
PLOT
KING'S
DOWNFALL

People deceive the king and his officers by their evil plots. They are all treacherous . . . Their hatred smoulders like the fire in an oven . . . (7:3, 4)

KINGS
ASSASSINATED

In the heat of their anger they murdered their rulers. Their kings have been assassinated one after another . . . (7:7)

This was the real Israel. This is what the Israelites got up to when they weren't queueing up to offer their sacrifices. They claimed to love God but totally rejected his commandments. There were 'Watergate-type' scandals every few weeks. There was a revolution or attempted coup every few months. In just two decades, Israel had six kings, and four of them were assassinated by their predecessors. It makes today's South American regimes look almost stable by comparison.

But Israel carried on regardless. It was so amazing. The people really believed that it did not matter. God would overlook this horrific catalogue of crime. God said: **'It never enters their heads that I will remember all this evil; but their sins surround them, and I cannot avoid seeing them.'** (7:2)

GRAND-DADDY IN THE SKY

The Israelites pictured God as a doting, absent-minded grandfather up in the sky. He might frown and wag his finger a bit, but he was too soft-hearted. He would never let his people suffer for long. 'Good old grandpa,' they thought. 'He'll forgive us in two or three days. Then he'll give us back our pocket money and sweets.' The Israelites had the wrong picture. Their image of God was as useless as a television on the blink. When the atmosphere is disturbed, a television picture becomes distorted. You cannot see it clearly. The Israelites had a similar problem. Their channel to God was distorted by sin. They could not see him because of the interference, so they finished up with a wrong image.

In chapter after chapter, Hosea had pictured God as a person. He is the Number One personality. He has personality features just like us. After all we are modelled in his image. Get his personality wrong and you end up with a different person – another god. Now the Israelites had got the very heart of God's personality wrong – his love. The love of a doting grand-daddy is a love that often spoils. God's love is a love that sometimes spanks. It is a love that cares so much that it is prepared to hurt to help.

God's love is sometimes a love that speaks/spanks.

Hosea was the right man to tell Israel about this love. His own love had been moulded by God. When he had married Gomer he was acting a part. He was in the role of God. So he understood about God's type of love. He loved Gomer so much that he too was prepared to be cruel to save her. First, there was the row over the illegitimate children. When hard words failed, he showed her the door. Even when Gomer returned to her senses and came home, Hosea starved her of sex. He wanted to teach her that love was more than a clinch in the dark. Gomer eventually got the message. She learnt what real love was all about. No doubt she became a better person for it.

Hosea had seen God's love in action. Gomer had been saved. But that was only a preview. Soon there would be a slow-motion, nationwide replay of this love. This time the central character would be God's own bride. The harsh words had already been spoken and Israel had paid no heed. Now she was to be thrown out of her homeland. She would be starved of all the normal ways of showing that she loved God. Her altars and temples would be smashed. As signs of love they had meant nothing anyway. Israel had offered cows and sheep to her husband just as Gomer had once given her body to Hosea. The motives were the same. Both wives wanted to keep their husbands quiet and happy while they carried on their love affairs. But God cried out: **'I want your constant love, not your animal sacrifices.'** (6:6)

WRONG GOD, WRONG RESPONSE

It was because Israel had a wrong picture of God, that her behaviour was wrong. After all, what was so special about an old fuddy-duddy? Why, you could buy his affections with a sad face, a few tears and the odd sacrifice. Israel's God was not even half a god! No wonder her response to him was only half-hearted. But the real God sees through Israel's love. He describes it to Hosea in three ways. His word pictures are very short but full of detail.

● **The people of Israel are like a half-baked loaf of bread. They rely on the nations around them.** (7:8)

God said that his bride had become mixed up with foreign lovers as thoroughly as yeast is stirred into flour in breadmaking. The yeast loses its identity in the flour. In the same way, Israel was totally absorbed into the life-style of other nations. She ends up half-baked. She was charred on one side and raw on the other. In other words, she was useless.

● **Israel flits about like a silly pigeon.** (7:11)

Israel was released into the world like a homing pigeon. She was to show the flight path back to God. But her homing mechanism had gone haywire. She had forgotten that she was supposed to home-in on God. Instead she flitted around the Middle East looking for a more attractive roost. She flew from Assyria to Egypt and other nations. She simply would not come home to God. She pleaded with foreigners for aid but, as God says: **'No one prays to me for help.'** (7:7)

The more Israel flapped, the less strength she had. Now the flighty bird would be netted in mid-air and taken away to be punished. (7:9-12)

● **Israel is as unreliable as a crooked bow.** (7:16)

Israel was God's strongbow. He wanted to use her to fire arrows of truth through the pagan armour of the world. But now the bow was badly buckled. It was fit for the scrap heap. Israel was supposed to convert the pagans but she had become as crooked as they were. She had let the pagans have their way with her. She worshipped what they worshipped, where they worshipped and how they worshipped. God said: **'I** wanted to save them, but their worship of me was false. They have not prayed to me sincerely, but instead they throw themselves down and wail as the heathen do . . . they gash themselves like pagans. What rebels they are!' (7:13-14)

Israel could certainly put on a great show. Some people might put on sack cloth and ashes to show their repentance. The Israelites preferred to do it the pagan way. They threw themselves down, wailed like lunatics and slashed their arms with jagged stones. It was a great show, all right, but that's all it was. When the show was over they forgot God and carried on as normal – murdering and mugging. So the Lord cried out: 'The people of Israel are doomed. They have left me and rebelled against me. They will be destroyed . . . Because their leaders talk arrogantly, they will die a violent death, and the Egyptians will laugh.' (7:13, 16)

Getting to know all
about him
(8:1-14)

Hosea's command performance before the royalty of Israel was drawing to an end. One thing was certain. There would be no encore! More likely the reaction would be, 'Don't call us, we'll call you.'

God's man had said a lot – too much for his VIP audience. But before he took his final bow, he made sure the message had gone home. He started to sum up, using more God-given words: **'Sound the alarm! Enemies are swooping down on my land like eagles! My people have broken the covenant . . . Even though they call me their God and claim . . . that they know me, they have rejected what is good.'** (8:1-3)

It could have been summed up in just one word – KNOW. The bride claimed to know her husband, but he knew better. And he could prove just how ignorant his bride was. Hosea makes a list of the evidence.

● **Israel has rejected good.** (8:3)

Good is the long way of spelling God. All that is good describes God. To reject good is to snub God.

The bride forgot the goodness of God when she threw away his Ten Commandments. These were the ten marriage rules and they ensured the good life.

● **Israel chose her own kings.**   (8:4)

Israel thought that her God was powerless. He simply could not cope. He could certainly not control her hefty muscle-bound neighbours like Assyria. Israel made up her mind. She needed a leader she could see and, if necessary, assassinate.

But she had forgotten something. Earthly kings were mere pawns in the hands of the heavenly king. Her own history could have reminded her. Look at the Egyptian Pharaoh. The King of Kings had really beaten him. He had sent plagues and performed miracles. He had even walled up the waters of the Red Sea.

● **Israel created her own gods.**   (8:4 – 6)

If at first you don't succeed, try another god. That was the way the Israelite mind worked. So the people collected together their gold and silver and went in to the god-manufacturing business.   (8:4) A gold bull was first off the production line. No – Israel had not completely lost her religious senses. She was surrounded by heathen worshippers. The bull was sacred to them. It stood for strength and fertility. That was what the Baal cult was all about. And these were just the items at the top of Israel's shopping list. She needed physical strength to fight off her strong neighbours, and fertile fields to hold off starvation. She was sorely tempted. These gods promised to deliver the goods. At last she could not resist any more. She transferred her affections.

It was so sad. Israel had closed her mind. She had forgotten all that God had done for her. He had

given her victories over her enemies. He had knocked
down the walls of Jericho and brought Israel to her
new homeland. And he had been a reliable bread-
winner too. He had made a daily delivery of manna
bread in the wilderness . . .

● **Israel rejected God's teachings.** (8:1, 12)

Israel was too wrapped up in the ways of other
nations. She looked at them and their beliefs and
forgot about God. His teaching became strange and
foreign. It was a case of, 'When in Canaan, do as the
Canaanites do.'

The Israelites were immigrants. They lived in a
strange land and saw new and different customs.
They wanted to belong so eventually they buried
their own traditions.

All immigrants meet the same problem. We can
see it today. In England there are many Asian
immigrants. When they first come, they find life
difficult. Perhaps they cannot speak much English.
Perhaps they find the climate cold and the food
strange. But soon they begin to adapt. They pick up a
new accent and learn new ways. And when English
people go to Australia, the same thing happens. They
change to fit their surroundings.

The Israelites did that. They changed drastically.
They had gone to Canaan for a purpose. They knew
the only true God. They were supposed to teach the
rest of the world about him. They were to convert
them. Instead, the Israelites themselves were con-
verted.

● **Israel forgot her maker.** (8:14)

The Israelites lost sight of their Creator. They forgot who he was. He had made the world and everything in it. He had put the stars in the sky and he looked after each of them. He was great and powerful. He was the living God. Yet the Israelites forgot what he was really like. He became a kind of Santa Claus in the sky. He was too big so they shrank him. They made him fit the tiny minds of men!

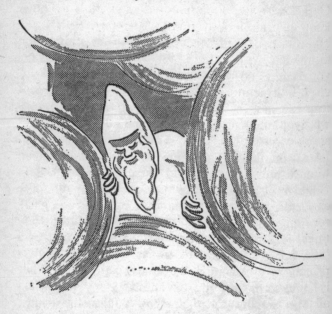

He became a kind of Santa Claus in the sky.

Israel then decided that her god was too small. He could not cope with her problems. So she was forced to act big herself. God declared: **'The people of Israel have built palaces, but they have forgotten their own Maker. The people of Judah have built fortified** cities . . .' (8:14) They might as well have built castles in the air. What protection would these give them when their enemies swooped down like eagles?

DID ISRAEL REALLY KNOW GOD?

This is the question. The answer must be: She knew God about as well as I know you, the reader. Israel knew that God existed. She knew one or two facts about him, but the rest was sheer fantasy. As for my knowledge about you, I know that you exist and that you are either male or female. That seems a safe start. I also know that you can read. But then I come to a full stop. I do not know what you look like or who you really are. I do not know whether you like sport or are good with your hands. And that was Israel's position with God. She knew him about as well as I know you.

Of course, I could invent a personality for you, just as Israel did for God. Firstly, I might think, 'My reader must be young and good-looking.' Then I might say, 'No, he is an older and wiser person' or 'She is a sentimental old lady.' By now you are probably feeling a little angry. 'Who does he think he is? Why should he think that I look like that?' After all, you have your own appearance and personality. You will feel resentful if I give you another.

But perhaps I have some excuse for doing this. I have never met you. I do not know you at all. Now Israel *did* know God. She was his bride. Yet she did exactly the same thing. She built up her own picture. She saw God as a soft-hearted old man who handed out treats. And so God felt angry.

71

SEX AND SACRIFICES

Israel's claim to know her husband would be a joke if her ignorance was not so serious. She loved a god but it was a false one. God's bride was behaving like Gomer. When Hosea's wife embraced him, she imagined that he was one of her lovers. Suppose your partner did the same thing. If you found out, how would you feel? God had found out and he had put up with it. He had been putting up with it for centuries.

But God's torment did not end there. When his bride tried to contact him through sacrifices, she was not just thinking of somebody else. She was also thinking of herself. Her sacrifices were not just to Baal, but also to her belly. The Lord put it this way: 'The Israelites **offer sacrifices to me, and eat the meat of the sacrifices.'** (8:13) Israel used God as an excuse to satisfy her own appetites, rather like Gomer used Hosea and her lovers. Israel was too wrapped up in her own pleasures. She would not spend time getting to know her husband. Soon she would have to pay for her deliberate ignorance.

IGNORANCE IS FAR FROM BLISS

Israel would soon find that her ignorance would lead to anything but bliss. She would discover that, in her ignorance, she had sown the seeds of her own destruction. Or as God put it: **'When they sow the wind, they will reap a storm.'** (8:7)

The old golden rule still applies, 'You reap what you sow.' Sow grain seeds and you reap grain. Sow evil deeds and you harvest only evil. Israel had sown useless seed. She had run for help to useless gods and equally useless nations. When harvest time came, she would be useless for God's purpose.

God uses two vivid word pictures to describe just how useless Israel was.

● **Israel . . . is as useless as a broken pot.** (8:8)

God had chosen Israel as a man might choose a beautiful jar. She was to carry his precious truth to the world. Now the jar was shattered. It was like pouring liquid gold into a broken milk bottle.

● **Stubborn as wild donkeys, the people of Israel go their own way.** (8:9)

Israel was a silly ass and God was the master to coax her along with many a carrot. That picture says much for God's amazing love and patience. It says even more about Israel's stubborn stupidity.

Israel was useless. She was only fit to be tossed aside on a rubbish heap and burnt. Or as the Lord said: **'I will send fire that will burn down their palaces and their cities.'** (8:14)

Speaking the truth
(9:1-10:15)

If a competition had been run to find the Most
Unpopular Personality of 8th Century BC Israel,
Hosea would have been favourite to take the title.
His royal debut turned him into a star overnight – a
falling star, the people hoped. He was bad news
wherever he went, and he knew it: ' "This prophet,"
you say, "is a fool . . ." You people hate me so much
because your sin is so great . . . You try to trap me like
a bird. In God's own land the people are the prophet's
enemies.' (9:7, 8)

From the people's point of view, Hosea was
Public Enemy Number One. They enjoyed their orgies
too much to give this loud-mouthed kill-joy a hearing.
And what is more, the people had little time for
prophets of doom. They only kicked Israel when she
was down. It was too much like treason! It did
nothing for the nation except shatter confidence. It
sent share prices tumbling, inflation soaring and
caused a run on the gold and silver currency.
Rumours of national disaster made life difficult.
Israel was poor. She needed help from Assyria who
operated an international monetary fund for its slave
nations. Rumours of doom were the last thing she
wanted, so Hosea was about as welcome as a saint in a
brothel.

Hosea had been acting a part. Now he shared the
fate of all unpopular actors. The audience hurled
things at him. In the theatre they usually throw

rotten tomatoes or bad eggs. In Israel the mobs fired abuse at Hosea. However the prophet was a fast-moving target. He did not stay too long in one place. His visiting card read, 'Have God, will travel.' Already, the royal city had vanished in the distance. It was just another stage in his whistle-stop tour of Israel. Now he was in Bethel, the religious centre of the North.

He rode into town in the middle of the harvest festival. Everyone in Bethel was having a good time. But when Hosea began to speak, the merry worshippers suddenly turned nasty. And no wonder! Hosea's previous speeches were bedtime stories compared to his harvest sermon in Bethel. His opening words set the tone: **'People of Israel, stop celebrating your festivals like pagans. You have turned away from your God.'** (9:1)

THE PARTY'S OVER

Usually Harvest is a time of thanksgiving. People say thank you in different ways. In some countries they take part of their crops to the local church. There they sing favourite hymns of praise to God. All seems peaceful and happy. Outside is the autumn sunshine; inside are the rich colours of the fruit and vegetables – all things bright and beautiful.

Things were different in Israel. Their harvest festival was an orgy of all things shady and ugly. The idol-worshippers wailed their way into the temple. They slashed their arms with chunks of rock. They had done bad things. Now they wanted to say sorry.

After the rock-ripping penance came the rip-roaring party. The wailing turned to laughter as the harvest offerings of corn and grapes were carried to the altar. First the harvest was offered to Baal . . . and then to the congregation's bellies in an orgy of food and drink. A good time was had by all, but the best was yet to come. The menfolk topped up with wine. Then they staggered as reverently as they could towards the temple cubicles. These housed the sacred prostitutes. It might be harvest time, but what about next year? Life had to go on. Baal had to supply that life. He must be encouraged and it was never too early to start. Well, that was their story, and they were sticking to it.

The presence of holy Hosea did not exactly help the festive spirit. Why did he have to be such an old-fashioned fuddy-duddy? Why didn't he let himself go and join the party? They could fix him up with a real beauty – if only he would sit down, shut up and sup up!

But a more powerful spirit controlled Hosea. The Spirit of God told him to stand up and speak up. When he spoke up, his audience quickly sobered up. His message was horribly stark and simple: 'The party's over. The hangover to end all hangovers is about to explode on your drunken minds. The days of wine, women and gods are past. The true God is at the door, and he is angry. You will lose everything near and dear.' Israel would first lose

FOOD

You have sold yourselves like prostitutes to the god Baal and have loved the corn you thought he paid you with! But soon you will not have enough corn and olive-oil, and there will be no wine. (9:1, 2)

i After the rock-ripping penance came the rip-roaring party.
*ii The presence of holy Hosea did not exactly help the festive
spirit.*

God's bride took her allowance of food and drink and then thanked her lover, Baal, instead of her husband. God was soon to prove who the real bread-winner was. His bride's allowance would be stopped. Next to go would be her

HOME

The people of Israel will not remain in the Lord's land, but will have to go back to Egypt. (9:3)

The bride would be thrown out of her homeland and be forced to return to a life of slavery. It would be just like the bad old days in Egypt. To Israelite ears, Egypt was a dirty five-letter word. It conjured up a miserable nightmare of chain-gang labour, back-breaking drudgery and whip-waving masters. This one word was enough to sober up Hosea's drunken audience. He goes on to tell them where this Egyptian-type slavery will take place, and that Israel will next lose

SPIRITUAL FOOD

The people . . . will have to go back to Egypt and will have to eat forbidden food in Assyria . . . They will not be able to make offerings of wine to the Lord, or bring their sacrifices to him. Their food will defile everyone who eats it, like food eaten at funerals. (9:3-4)

The Israelites would be taken into exile in Assyria, and scattered across that vast empire. There, they would have to beg or borrow food. That presented a big problem. The food would be unclean. It would not be crawling with bacteria. It might even be very fresh. But the Israelites would not eat it. They had their laws. All food was unclean until at least some of it had been offered to the Lord in his house. The fruit might be straight off the tree but the Israelites could not touch it. It must be blessed first. It was like getting the stamp of approval from the Divine Health Authority. But soon, Israel would be in exile hundreds of miles from home. She would not be able to visit the Lord's house. How could she gain his approval? She would be like funeral mourners. They were not allowed to enter God's house because they had been with dead men. People thought they were unclean too.

Assyrian food might satisfy their physical hunger, but it would contain no spiritual vitamins. The Israelites would next lose

RELIGION

God will break down their altars . . . The people . . . will mourn the loss of the gold bull at Bethel . . . The idol will be carried off to Assyria as tribute to the great emperor . . . The hilltop shrines . . . where the people of Israel worship idols, will be destroyed. (10:2-8)

Israel went mad on idol-worship. It might have been a load of superstitious mumbo-jumbo, but it ruled the people's lives nevertheless. No expense was spared. Religious centres were a cross between a miniature Fort Knox and a high-class jewellers. The 24-carat bull was surrounded by precious stones and silverware. They had set up in competition with the stars in the sky.

But a robbery was about to take place. Soon the

religious trimmings would be carried off by the Assyrian invaders. Israel would be stripped of religion and riches and left in rags. Next to go would be her . . .

CHILDREN

Israel's greatness will fly away like a bird, and there will be no more children born to them, no more women pregnant, no more children conceived. But even if they did bring up children, I would take them away and not leave one alive. When I abandon these people, terrible things will happen to them. (9:11, 12)

Next in importance to religion came children. Mr Modern Man measures his importance by the size of his car. Mr Average Israelite's greatness came from the size of his family. A son was *the* status symbol in Israel. Not only could a son help on the farm, but he was also a guarantee. If a man had a son, he would not be forgotten when he died. Israelites firmly believed that they lived on in their sons and grandsons. That was the average man's idea of eternal life. The more sons he had, the better his chances of survival. And boys kept the family name alive. That was important too. So if you had no sons, it was a fate worse than death.

This explains why the temple prostitutes were so popular. When the Israelites produced new life in their wombs they were encouraging Baal to produce new life in two other directions. The first was in the land and the second in the loins of the menfolk.

An Israelite would rather have suffered from anything than sterility!

So the men of Bethel turned nasty. And now we can understand why. Hosea had made some frightening claims. The Israelites would not be able to have children. The men would be impotent and the women barren. And just suppose a child was born! Hosea announced that it would be hunted down and killed. It was adding insult to injury. (9:13)

In other words, Israel was going to get what she deserved. And it would be her own fault. She was going to end up like the majority of prostitutes – barren! When women take to street-walking, they are in for trouble. They abuse their bodies so much that often they cannot bear babies. Israel had sold herself as a prostitute. She had taken false lovers. Now she would be barren.

Next to go would be

LEADERS

These people will soon be saying, 'We have no king because we did not fear the Lord. But what could a king do for us anyway?' They utter empty words and make false promises and useless treaties . . . Israel's king will be carried off, like a chip of wood on water. (10:3, 4, 7)

Israel wanted strong leaders. She thought they were the most important thing. She would go to all lengths to get them. And she did. She waged civil war and committed wholesale murder. Then the blow came. Assyria conquered Israel. Her top men were rounded up and deported. But at least Assyria had replaced them with puppet leaders, like King Hoshea.

Leaders, even with strings attached to them, were better than none at all.

'But soon they too will go,' says Hosea. 'Hoshea and all the king's men will vanish like useless spent matchsticks floating down the gutter.'

Israel was in for a rude awakening. She might have kings but she was no better off. Her kings were all talk and no action. They were like many a politician. They promised the world, but delivered only a whorl – of hot air. Soon the people would acknowledge the Lord as their true king, but by then it would be too late.

Last to go would be

MILITARY MIGHT

Because you trusted in your chariots and in the large numbers of your soldiers, war will come to your people, and all your fortresses will be destroyed. It will be like the day when King Shalman destroyed the city of Betharbel in battle, and mothers and their children were crushed to death.   (10:13, 14)

Israel shrank her Lord down to the size of a tin god. Then she had a shock. She had to rely on herself and her own defences. Israel lived by the chariot. Now she would die by it. Fortresses would collapse as though they were built of playing cards, and soldiers would tumble over like tenpins in a bowling alley.

The mention of Betharbel must have sent a shiver through Hosea's audience. They remembered Shalman. He was King Shalmaneser III of Assyria. He had come with his army and killed all the children in the city. It had been a bloodbath. Conquering kings usually did such things. If you got rid of the children, you destroyed a troublesome nation. Now Hosea gives a warning. This will happen to Israel, because of the great evil she had done.   (10:15)

The party was well and truly over. Israel would lose everything. Even her prized possessions would go. The shock would be so great that she would beg to have her suffering and shame ended. **The people will call out to the mountains, 'Hide us!' and to the hills, 'Cover us!'   (10:8)**

A BEAUTIFUL BEGINNING

Israel's end is a horror story. Hosea does not spare the ghastly details. In fact, he makes them sound worse because he goes back to the beginning. Then everything was beautiful. At the start, Israel was ripe and ready to live happily ever after with her heavenly husband.

SHE WAS RIPE

The Lord says, 'When I first found Israel, it was like finding grapes growing in the desert. When I first saw your ancestors, it was like seeing the first ripe figs of the season.'   (9:10)

Here was God's world. He had planted it in the universe. He had gazed at it in love. Once it had been a garden of beauty. Then disaster had come. Man had run riot, like an ugly weed. He had ruined everything in sight. The garden became a wilderness, and eventually shrivelled and died. Yet God could still see signs of life. Abraham, the ancestor of Israel, was still faithful to him. It was like finding a juicy young grapevine in the desert. With love and care, God nursed it, fed it, trained it. Then he transplanted it into the heart of a dead world. He planned that the vine would spread out and cover the wasteland with new life. Instead, it turned in on itself. As it grew it kept the fruit and goodness to itself. Hosea puts it this way: **'The people of Israel were like a grapevine that was full of grapes. The more prosperous they were, the more altars they built. The more productive their land was, the more beautiful they made the sacred stone pillars they worship.'** (10:1)

The garden became a wilderness.

Israel lost her ripeness the moment she set foot in her new homeland. **When they came to Mount Peor, they began to worship Baal, and soon became as disgusting as the gods they loved. (9:10)**

God's people had marched into Canaan. They were ripe to show the world the way back to God. Within days, thousands of the men were making love to the local women. Later, they went with the women to a sacrificial feast in honour of Baal (Numbers 25).

Soon after this, came the Gibeah affair. **The Lord says, 'The people of Israel have not stopped sinning against me since the time of their sin at Gibeah.' (10:9)**

Gibeah was three miles north of Jerusalem. It stood out in the minds of the Israelites as the gas chambers of Auschwitz haunt modern Jews. Here a Benjamite raped a priest's wife. A dreadful war of revenge followed and the tribe of Benjamin was almost wiped out. (Judges 19, 20)

Once Israel was ripe. Then came Mount Peor and Gibeah and she turned rotten.

SHE WAS READY

The Lord says . . . 'Israel was once like a well-trained young cow, ready and willing to thresh grain. But I decided to . . . harness her for harder work . . . I said, "Plough new ground for yourselves, plant righteousness, and reap the blessings that your devotion to me will produce!" ' (10:11, 12)

Israel ploughed into her new ground, the new homeland in Canaan. She was supposed to plant new good seed, but the opposite happened. **You planted evil and reaped its harvest. (10:13)**

Once Israel was ripe and ready. Now she was rotten and unreliable. In fact, she had been useless ever since she entered her new homeland. Because of this, says Hosea, she would lose everything. She would lose her physical and spiritual food, her home, religion and riches, her greatness and children, her leaders and her military might. And it would all happen in a horrific bloodbath.

Hosea turns his back on his audience of drunks. He hurls a final threat from the Lord himself: **'That is what will happen to you, people of Bethel, because of the terrible evil that you have done. As soon as the battle begins, the king of Israel will die.' (10:15)**

Bigger than all of us
(11:1-11)

First, the bad news: Israel will drown in her own
bloodbath. Now for the good news. Well, that is what
Hosea's closing words at Bethel are all about. Today,
we know them simply as Chapter Eleven. But what a
dry, dead way of describing those 300 words!
Together they spell out the greatest thing on earth –
God's never-ending love. They deserve to be inscribed
in gold and decorated with diamonds on a mother-of-
pearl background. That is how precious they are. If
ever Hosea was set to music, this is where a multi-
trumpet fanfare would stop the show.

Take away these love words and the rest of Hosea's
news can appear under one depressing headline:
ISRAEL, GO TO HELL. But this chapter of love
turns that dismal message on its head: 'HELL IS TO
GO . . . at least as far as Israel is concerned.'

And to prove this, Hosea takes his audience on a
fantastic voyage. They go right into the heart of God.
It is a journey of discovery, for it was largely un-
explored territory for the men of Hosea's day.

Hosea himself had taken previous audiences on
short excursions. He had guided them round the
tender heart of a loving husband for his unfaithful
wife. He had shown them a suffering heart that could
absorb the hurt and hate of a thousand years and yet
still go on pumping out love. He had revealed to
them a caring heart. This heart was really concerned
about the future of Israel. It was prepared to be cruel
to be kind.

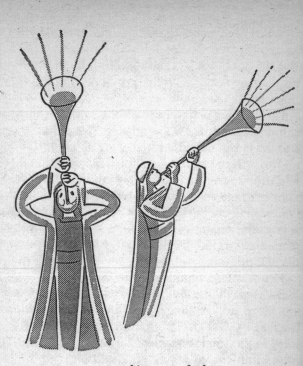

. . . a multi-trumpet fanfare.

But now Hosea says, 'Let me take you further. You haven't seen anything yet.'

THE BIG HEART

Let us look at the love which pours from the heart of God. It is as intense as the passion of young lovers. It has more stamina than a dozen Darby and Joan pairs. And yet when you have said all this, it is still only half the love story. God's heart is so much bigger.

When Man wants to describe real love, he talks of a happily married couple. It is the best picture he has. But it does not do justice to the one-and-only partnership between God and his bride. When Hosea talks about God, he is as handicapped as a painter. An artist can work wonders. On a piece of canvas he can paint a scene. He can give an idea of the colour and the movement. But he has to stop there. It is only an image. He cannot reproduce the real thing. He might be a great genius; he might have the gifts of Leonardo da Vinci, Van Gogh and Picasso but he is limited. His work is still only a pale copy of the real thing. Hosea paints with words. Yet his man-wife picture is a flat, two-dimensional affair compared to the 3D love that God has for his bride.

The marriage picture can give a false impression. Ideas of marriage change. In many countries, women are 'liberated'. They burn their bras and look for tough jobs. They become welders or dockers. They look at marriage with different eyes. It becomes a partnership and links two equals. Each person has to rely on the other. In Hosea's day, a wife had little more status than the family camel but she could still exist as a separate person without her husband.

Now this is not the picture of God's partnership with Israel. For one thing, Israel could never be equal to God, nor did God ever have to rely on his bride. The opposite was true. Israel was like a babe in arms. She was wholly dependent on God. So Hosea changes the picture. He gives his audience a wider view of God's love. It is like a parent's love for a child. Israel is a helpless baby who is tied to God's apron strings. **The Lord says,**

'When Israel was a child, I loved him . . .
But the more I called to him,
  the more he turned away from me.
My people sacrificed to Baal;
  they burnt incense to idols.
Yet I was the one who taught Israel to walk.
  I took my people up in my arms . . .
I drew them to me with affection and love.
  I picked them up and held them to my cheek;
  I bent down to them and fed them.' (11:1-4)

This relationship is bigger than any we have ever met
on earth. It is bigger than all of us. There are many
pictures of human love. If your mind were an art
gallery, it would soon be full. But it might just as well
be empty. The whole collection could not illustrate
God's love. It is just too big. It is out of this world
and the words of this world can only begin to hint at
the real thing.

THE STORMY HEART

Hosea now brings his audience to the centre of God's
heart. Suddenly, the calm journey is over. They are
in the grip of a hurricane. The world has never seen
such a storm. God's justice and love appear to have
declared war on one another.

God's justice declares: **'They refuse to return to me
. . . War will sweep through their cities . . . It will
destroy my people . . . They will cry out because of the
yoke that is on them, but no one will lift it from
them.'** (11:5-7)

God's love replies:

> 'How can I give you up, Israel?
>   How can I abandon you?
> Could I ever destroy you as I did Admah,
>   or treat you as I did Zeboiim?
> My heart will not let me do it!
>   My love for you is too strong.'   (11:8)

The big heart of God is caught up in an almighty tug of war. Justice tugs the heart strings one way. It demands that Israel gets what she deserves. She should be destroyed like Admah and Zeboiim. God had flattened those cities long ago. They had been dens of sin like their neighbours Sodom and Gomorrah. But love tugs equally as hard in the opposite direction. Love digs in its heels and pulls for mercy.

What an impossible contest! If justice wins, can God any longer be called a God of love? And if love wins, what about justice? And justice is important. If there is no justice in the heart of the universe then there is no justice anywhere. London's Old Bailey might as well shut up shop and give the Underworld its blessing. America's Supreme Court can stop judging presidents and people alike and adjourn indefinitely.

And so the tug of war forces battle on. Hosea's audience waits and watches. What will be the outcome? How can such an impossible contest be decided? And then, as suddenly as it started, the storm dies. The contest is over.

> 'I will not punish you in my anger;
>   I will not destroy Israel again.'   (11:9)

God has decided. When Hosea first received this

message from God, a huge question mark must have
hovered in his mind. His faith in the justice of God
must have been tested to the outer limits. Nevertheless, he passed on the message. He must not ask why
or how. He had to do the will of God. He carried out
the will of God because he knew God. He knew how
God had behaved in the past. On that form he was
prepared to trust him for the future. God had made
his decision. There was no more to be said . . . at
least, not for another 700 years.

THE SATISFIED HEART

It was only after seven centuries that God added a
word of explanation. The Word took the form of
flesh and blood. It was his son, Jesus Christ. The son
was sent into the world with a job to do. He had to
meet the demands both of justice and love. He had to
make sure that the penalty for man's crimes was paid
in full. Only that would satisfy justice. But he also
had to save man from death. Only that would meet
the demands of love.

At 3 o'clock on a dismal Friday afternoon, Jesus
Christ hung by nails from a rough wooden cross on a
hill called Skull. On the stroke of the hour he cried
out in triumph: 'It is finished!' And with these words
he slumped forward dead.

'Mission impossible' was stamped 'mission success-
ful'. In his love, Jesus had taken man's place on
execution hill. He had paid the penalty himself for
man's sins. And only he could have done it. Love and
justice met perfectly and harmoniously in God's son.

It was a perfect solution. It took the impossible

strain out of the tug of war in God's heart. Of course, it must be stressed that it only seemed impossible to the human spectator. Nothing is impossible to God. He had provided the answer to this problem before the world was even created. You can read about this in the book of Revelation, Chapter 13.

However, Hosea did not know about that. He would certainly have let on if he had. But he was happy to pass on God's message, whether he understood it fully or not. He was convinced that God knew what he was doing.

The faithful Hosea went on to show his audience yet another quality of God's love.

A SUPERHUMAN HEART

'I will not destroy Israel again.
For I am God and not man.
I, the Holy One, am with you.
I will not come to you in anger.' (11:9)

If God's heart had been human, things would have been very different. The child Israel would not have survived. No father could have coped with such behaviour. Israel would have become another battered baby. And no husband could have put up with such a wife. If God had loved his bride with human affection, Israel would have been divorced long ago. She could not sleep around and still remain married.

But God could cope, says Hosea. He is superhuman. He is the Holy One. He is completely separate from man and the ways of man's heart.

The human heart beats many million times, flutters, and then splutters out like a soggy, worn-out sponge. And human love sometimes gives up even sooner. But the love of God's eternal heart is everlasting.

The human heart becomes scarred. It gets hurt and so it wants to defend itself. It builds up barriers until even love is shut out. But God's heart does not do this. He refuses to protect himself. Instead, he carries on loving. This was a love-without-defences. It was a never-ending love. It was a love that sent Jesus to one of the most brutal deaths man has invented. No wonder somebody once called God 'the chief sufferer of the universe'.

A STERN HEART

The message rings out loud and clear: 'God's love will save Israel.' But if Hosea's audience thought that they were to be let off lightly by a love-struck God, then they needed to think again. This good news chapter in no way cancels out the bad news of the other ten.

It was true that God had promised that he would not destroy Israel. Nor would he punish her in his anger. But she would certainly be punished in his love. As we have already seen, **War will sweep through their cities . . . (11:6)**

God's love is not sloppy sentiment. It is a fatherly love and it must act sternly to save his son from foolishness. If you had a son, would you let him play with fire? If you did, could you say you really loved him? Love would make you warn him. At first you would do it gently. But if he continued, you would use harsher words. If they failed, a few sharp smacks might teach him the error of his ways. Maybe you might even let him burn his fingers. Better that than to see him burnt alive. But even this might not work. Your child might be really captivated by fire. He might even become an arsonist. As you survey the charred remains of his school, there is only one remedy left. You must send him away from home. He will have to face his punishment and then be trained properly.

If you had a son, would you let him play with fire?

Israel had reached this stage. God's son had become completely captivated by crime. Now only exile would bring him to his senses.

But the story does not end there. Hosea finishe
this love chapter with God's words of promise fo
Israel: 'My people will follow me when I roar like a
lion at their enemies. They will hurry to me from the
west. They will come from Egypt, as swiftly as birds
and from Assyria, like doves. I will bring them to thei
homes again. I, the Lord, have spoken.' (11:10, 11)

One day the stern, lion-hearted God would call hi
people back home. The lion would first tear Israel to
pieces and carry her off (5:14). But when she had
learnt her lesson, the lion would turn on her enemie
and she would be free. Then she could come hurry
ing home from every corner of the earth.

For Hosea, all this lay in the future. But for u
today, some of it is a matter of history. Israel wa
dragged off into exile by Assyria in 721 BC. The
same thing happened to Judah 150 years later. Sh
fell to the new regime of Babylon. It was only afte
years of exile that God's people were repatriated. I
540 BC a new Babylonian emperor came to power
He had a different foreign policy and decided to send
the refugees back to their homeland once again

Israel's story has a happy ending. But this is only
part of it. There is to be an even greater finale – bu
for that, we have to wait to the end of Hosea's book

None of this
(12:1-14:3)

Long and faithful service deserves a reward. When a
good worker finishes his job he should get a pat on
the back and a gold watch – or even a golden hand-
shake! Hosea deserved such treatment. For 40 years
he had toured Israel's market towns. He had faced
the roar of the crowd. Now the last lap was over. No
more would he be laughed out of town – or thrown
out! The last laugh would soon be his.

Already, Assyria's invasion forces were massing
along the northern borders of Israel. They were
about to prove, once and for all, that Hosea knew
what he was talking about.

Israel's puppet king, Hoshea, had been increasingly tugging against the Assyrian strings. He was tired
of dancing to a foreign tune. Now he wanted to call
his own. He wanted freedom. Meanwhile, north of
the border, Assyria's Shalmaneser was growing
impatient. Now, when he pulled a string, the puppet
refused to jump to it. Just one more excuse! That was
all he needed. Then he would tear both string and
puppet into tiny pieces. Hosea knew it was only a
matter of time. Soon Israel's king would provide just
such an excuse.

Hosea looked back on his life with mixed feelings.
He had done all that was asked of him. He had
delivered the message in a thousand places, even
when people had tried to drown it with laughter. But
there was little to show for the work of a lifetime.

Israel was still as bad as ever. Soon the prophet would die, and yet it was vital that the message should live on. Who knows! Israel might still repent at the eleventh hour.

Israel's puppet king had been increasingly pulling against the Assyrian strings.

With this in mind Hosea sat down, sharpened his reed-point pen and, for the last time, took down his sheep's horn of ink. His last job would be to shrink a million words into a few glaring headlines. This generation might be deaf to his message, but perhaps the next one would take notice.

Eleven chapters are now safely on paper. There is nothing new to say. But still God's prophet cannot rest. He must make doubly sure his readers get the message. It must come over loud and clear. There must be no mistake. And so he begins to sum up the main points. He goes back over Israel's life of crime as though he is a lawyer. He sums up the case for the prosecution. First comes . . .

The Lord says, 'The people of Israel have surrounded me with lies and deceit, and the people of Judah are still rebelling against me, the faithful and holy God. Everything that the people of Israel do from morning to night is useless and destructive. Treachery and acts of violence increase among them. They make treaties with Assyria and do business with Egypt.'

The Lord has an accusation to bring against the people of Judah; he is also going to punish Israel for the way her people act. (11:12-12:2)

The charge has been read. Now Hosea turns to the evidence to back up the accusation. And for this he opens the history books.

EVIDENCE FOR THE PROSECUTION

The beginning: The nation of Israel was born selfish. She had a selfish father too. He was one of the best con men in the business. Jacob was a small-time crook who grabbed for the big time. He was even grabbing before he was born. In a few words, Hosea sums up his story. You can read it in more detail in Genesis 25-33. The Israelites' **ancestor Jacob struggled with his twin brother Esau while the two of them were still in their mother's womb; when Jacob grew up, he fought against God – he fought against an angel and won. He wept and asked for a blessing. And at Bethel God came to our ancestor Jacob and spoke with him. (12:3-4)**

Jacob was a pusher. Even in the womb he struggled. He wanted to be born first so he grabbed at his twin Esau's head. In those days it was important to be the first son out of the womb. It meant fame and fortune. The oldest son inherited twice as much as his other brothers, and eventually won social standing as head of the family.

But this birth race had an even bigger prize. The winner would become the father of a great nation. God had made his promise. Of course, the minus-one-day-old Jacob knew nothing of promises. He was just a baby grabbing at life. But once a grabber, always a grabber. Jacob might have lost that particular race. He was pipped at the post. A few precious seconds robbed him of first place. But he wasn't beaten. He set out to make up for lost time and he used lots of tricks and schemes. The Old Testament tells us all about them.

Actually, he could have saved his energy. He was meant to win. God had planned it that way. Jacob would get the property and the promises. He might not have been born first but he became the firstborn. (Genesis 25:23) He had only to wait and God would have handed it all to him on a plate. But Jacob wanted to do things his own way.

A new beginning: God finally caught up with Jacob after 20 years of trickery. And this time Jacob met his match. He fought a strange wrestling bout with an angel of God. Jacob came off worst. He was crippled, but the contest turned him into a new man. God won him over. Later, at Bethel, he met Jacob and gave him his full blessing and a new beginning. At last Jacob began to do God's thing instead of his own. No longer was he Jacob, the grabber. He was renamed Israel, the one who strives with God. (Genesis 32)

Back to square one: Now Israel and his descendants had a job to do. They were to help God. They had to strive with him in the pagan world and change it. But the plan went wrong. By Hosea's time, the only thing the Israelites were striving for was themselves. In fact Israel had changed back into Jacob. Israel had become a nation of grabbers. She had become just as bad as the people she was supposed to convert. **The Lord says, 'The people of Israel are as dishonest as the Canaanites; they love to cheat their customers with false scales. "We are rich," they say. "We've made a fortune. And no one can accuse us of getting rich dishonestly." '** (12:7, 8)

'Why shouldn't I hoodwink the customer? What's wrong in that?' thought Mr Average Israelite. Everybody finger-tipped the scales, so why all the fuss? It was no worse than fiddling your tax returns, or pinching odds and ends from work as an extra perk. Everybody did it! Where was the harm? The Israelites became caught up with this Canaanite way of thinking. Eventually they could not tell a right from a wrong.

The beginning of the end: Hosea continues to sum up for the prosecution. Daylight robbery was only one of Israel's crimes. Much more serious was her idolatry. This was the root of all her evil. This was the beginning of her sad end. **The people sinned by worshipping Baal, and for this they will die.** (13:1) The God of Israel might be able to roll back the Red Sea waters; he might have proved himself a reliable breadwinner in the Wilderness; he might even be a battle winner for Israel. But could he grow crops? Could he make the rain fall at the right time? In fact, could Israel trust this God now that she had left the harsh desert and settled down on the farm? To put it bluntly, did a change of life-style demand a change of god?

An attractive competitor was waiting in the wings. It was the local fertility god, Baal. When it came to farming, he seemed to have green fingers for the land was already overflowing with the good things of life. The Canaanites seemed to have picked a winner. Why look further? Why take a bigger gamble than was necessary? Better the god with experience than the one without! Before long, the Israelites began redirecting their sacrifices to Baal. Of course, they had to carve his image first . . . **They still keep on sinning by making metal images to worship – idols of silver, designed by human minds, made by human hands . . . How can men kiss those idols? (13:2)**

You can almost hear Hosea's sarcasm. Imagine it! Fancy bowing and scraping before a lump of metal or wood! How foolish can you get? The Israelites had forgotten one simple fact: God makes man, not the other way round.

The last straw: The Israelites' mistrust of God led to worse behaviour, says Hosea. **They make treaties with Assyria, and do business with Egypt. (12:1)**

Israel had a treaty with God. He would protect her if she trusted him and kept his laws. This was the agreement he had made on Mount Sinai. But when Israel's neighbours turned awkward, she lost faith in her partner's abilities to cope. Instead of relying on God's power, she invented her own power game. She played one neighbour off against the other; Assyria against Egypt and vice versa.

Israel's kings were in charge of the power game. And that was yet another crime. God was supposed to be king of Israel. But Israel was unable to see him, so cried out for a flesh and blood ruler. She wanted a leader whom she could touch; somebody who could stand up and rally the nation together in times of crises. God was angry. Yet he allowed Israel to choose a human king. He wanted to teach her a lesson and this was the only way. Soon she would realize her foolishness. How could she trust anyone less than God?

Hosea rests his case. He has laid out the evidence. Israel has committed daylight robbery. She has doubted God's power and dethroned him in favour of a human king and a pagan god. She has even preferred her double dealings with foreign kings instead of dealing straightforwardly with the King of Kings. This was the last straw. Look at Hosea's closing words. They are a sharp warning. None of Israel's crimes would be forgotten. **Israel's sin and guilt are on record, and the records are safely stored away. (13:12)**

EVIDENCE FOR THE DEFENCE?

The prosecution has had its say. Now it is Israel's turn. She has to take the stand in her own defence. However there is just one problem. Israel has no defence to put forward. She does not even have an excuse. She has had too many warnings for that, says the great judge. '. . . **through the prophets I gave my people warnings . . .**' Their **ancestor Jacob had to flee to Mesopotamia, where, in order to get a wife, he**

103

The prosecution has had its say.

worked for another man and took care of his sheep
The Lord sent a prophet to rescue the people of Israel
from slavery in Egypt and to take care of them . . .
(12:10-13)

For the last time, Hosea turns the pages of history
to make his point. The Israelites were God's special
flock, so he sent shepherds to guide and protect them
But no shepherd ever had a more stubborn flock to
handle. The Israelites won all the prizes at that game
They were constantly straying into danger.

Hosea turns back to the Jacob story. He shows
just how hard God's shepherds were made to work
Jacob was the crook who made good with a shepherd's crook, but he never worked harder in his life

He had to. His wife depended upon it. Jacob wanted to marry Rachel but he had to pay for her. Laban made him look after his sheep for 14 years. A wedding ring is cheap in comparison! (Genesis 29-31)

In just the same way, God's shepherds were made to work long and hard. Hosea gives Moses as the best example. He led God's flock out of the troubles of Egypt and took care of them for 40 years. Often the Israelites ignored him, as they did with all God's shepherds. Today we call these men prophets. They tried everything to turn Israel away from danger. But they failed. The reason for failure was simple: the Israelites refused to listen. Sometimes the prophets were shouted down. Other times they were stoned or killed. One was even sawn in two. (Hebrews 11:37)

THE SENTENCE

Israel has no defence or excuse. She is guilty and she knows it. Now comes the judgement. 'I will make you live in tents again, as you did when I came to you in the desert. (12:9) The altars . . . will become piles of stones . . .' (12:11) . . . These people will disappear like morning mist . . . like smoke from a chimney . . . (13:3) 'I will attack you like a bear that has lost her cubs, and I will tear you open. (13:8) Bring on your plagues, death! Bring on your destruction, world of the dead! . . . (13:14) Her people will die in war; babies will be dashed to the ground, and pregnant women will be ripped open.' (13:16)

The crimes have been committed, the evidence submitted, the verdict given, and the sentence passed. Only one thing remains: the execution! But wait a minute! Something is missing. Court scenes end with an eleventh-hour plea for mercy. Will this one be different? No, Israel's case is no exception. She still has a chance. Even after a life of robbery, murder, treachery, violence and idolatry, Israel can still escape death and live. Hosea explains. **Israel has a chance to live, but is too foolish to take it – like a child about to be born, who refuses to come out of the womb. (13:13)**

Israel can avoid punishment. She has only to say one word and mean it – 'Sorry.' Hosea makes it as easy as possible for her to do this. He writes out an apology for her. He pleads, **'Return to the Lord and let this prayer be your offering to him: "Forgive all our sins and accept our prayer, and we will praise you as we have promised. Assyria can never save us, and war horses cannot protect us. We will never again say to our idols that they are our God. O Lord, you show mercy to those who have no one else to turn to." '** (14:2-3)

How hard it is to say 'Sorry'! We now know that it was impossible for Israel. Shortly after Hosea had written these words, the Assyrian forces attacked. They ripped Israel to pieces in one of the most horrific conquests of ancient times. Justice had been done. The punishment had been made to fit Israel's crimes. But that was not the end. There will be no sad ending to God's love story.

A happy ending
(14:4-9)

Israel will be torn to pieces. Babies will be dashed to the ground. Pregnant women will be ripped open. It is strong stuff but believable. Two world wars and a Vietnam have shown us worse. But we still have problems. Take a look at the ending. Modern men still find it difficult to accept. Hosea's last words about God and Israel add up to one well-known saying, '. . . and they will live happily ever after.' Today, a sceptical world sneers at the happy endings:

'Fairy-tale fantasy,' writes the TV critic.
'Wishful thinking,' shrugs the man in the street.
'Cockeyed optimism,' warbles the singer.

But we are not dealing with fantasy. That is one charge we simply cannot make. In the last 13 chapters God and his writers have shown us something different. Their words are more down-to-earth than if all today's kitchen-sink dramas were rolled into one miserable epic.

God has proved himself to be a realist, and Hosea is no dreamer either. Nevertheless, they still predict a happy ending for Israel. In fact, life will not only be a bed of roses, but also of blossoming flowers, beautiful evergreen trees and scented shrubs. That is how God sums up the happy ending. He says:

I will be to the people of Israel
like rain in a dry land. (14:5)

This is the promise of new life for Israel. Without God there is death. Israel had thrown God out long ago, and now she was as dead as a dusty desert. But one day God will come raining down on the Israelites to make them **blossom like flowers . . . (14:5)** Ugly, dead Israel will become beautiful, like a full-blown rose. Israel the clumsy sinner will be as delicate as the scented petals of a lily. Not only this, Israel will be **firmly rooted like the trees of Lebanon . . . (14:5)** The roots of the giant cedars of Lebanon sink to rock. They are almost as long as the tree is tall. You don't dig up a cedar of Lebanon. You blast it with dynamite. That is how firmly rooted Israel will be in her God.

But there is more to come. Israel will be **alive with new growth, and beautiful like olive trees. (14:6)** Israel's new life will be beautiful. It will also be everlasting like the evergreen olives. They are like a permanent green scarf on the shoulders of dry, dusty Palestine.

The Israelites will also be **fragrant like the cedars of Lebanon. Once again they will live under God's protection . . . flourish like a garden . . . be fruitful like a vineyard . . . be as famous as the wine of Lebanon. (14:6, 7)** Israel will no longer stink like a cheap-scented prostitute. She will have about her a natural perfume, the aroma of God. She will also be as fruitful in her love as the best vineyards are with their grapes. She will produce only the best, like the vintage wines of Lebanon – the champagne of the 8th Century BC!

Finally, the Israelites **will have nothing more to do with idols . . .** God **will shelter them;** he is **the source of all their blessings. (14:8)**

Israel will become beautiful like a full-blown rose.

Just as soil is the source of life for flowers, so God is the life-giving source of Israel. But Israel had performed a do-it-yourself transplant. She had uprooted herself from God and crawled into poisonous beds. God would have been well within his rights to say, 'You've made your own beds, now you can die in them.' But he loved Israel too much for that. One day he would save the withering, shrivelled-up Israel and transplant her back into himself, her natural source of life.

POSTSCRIPT

Hosea sits back. His message is completed, his summary is at an end. And yet still he cannot resist picking up his pen once more. This time, he adds a P.S. **May those who are wise understand what is written here, and may they take it to heart. The Lord's ways are right, and righteous people live by following them, but sinners stumble and fall because they ignore them. (14:9)** If you have any sense at all, says Hosea, you will sit up and take notice of what God has said. If you have real wisdom, you will get the message.